Dance, Art and Aesthetics

Distributed By
Princeton Book Co. Publishers
P.O. Box 109, Princeton, NJ 08540

Dance, Art and Aesthetics

Betty Redfern

Dance Books Ltd
9 Cecil Court, London WC2

First published in 1983 by Dance Books Ltd., 9 Cecil Court,
London WC2N 4EZ
ISBN 0 903102 73 0

Design and production in association with
Book Production Consultants, 47 Norfolk Street, Cambridge

Printed by The Burlington Press (Cambridge) Ltd,
Foxton, Cambridge

Contents

Preface

Introductory texts on aesthetics are usually able to proceed on the assumption that those approaching the subject will do so with an interest in and some background of philosophy. Today, however, numbers of students with little initial interest or background of this kind are required to study aesthetics as part of courses in dance or dance and related activities. Such students are further handicapped by the paucity of aesthetic enquiry in this realm. Nevertheless it cannot be hived off from the rest of aesthetics, and indeed there is much to be gained by first becoming familiar with more general issues.

Taking the dance as the principal focus of concern, this book therefore aims to present a selection of topics in aesthetics in such a way as to highlight the wider philosophical problems that are inevitably involved, indicating some of the changes and developments that have taken place in aesthetic thought during the last thirty years or so, and introducing some of the work of well-known writers in the field. It is thus chiefly of an expository character, and quotations and references are used liberally throughout in an attempt to promote understanding of philosophical argument and assist further reading.

At its core are questions to do with the nature and value of art, the character of aesthetic experience and the justification of aesthetic appraisals – questions traditionally at the centre of aesthetic enquiry, but still well to the fore in contemporary debate. The nature of the connection between art and the aesthetic, however, which tends to receive less attention than it would seem to deserve, is also explored, particularly from the point of view of the diversity of dance forms and of developments in Post-Modern art.

A major topic to which specific consideration has deliberately not been given here is that of expressiveness and the expression of feeling; for although much remains in need of further investigation in this connection, both in relation to the arts and beyond, this is an area that has already received a fair amount of attention from philosophers interested in the dance.

My indebtedness to certain authors will be evident from the text; but over a period of time ideas sometimes take root in one's mind in a way that renders it

1

difficult to trace their origins, and I therefore gratefully acknowledge anyone on whose work I may have drawn without having been aware of so doing.

There are also a number of individuals who, in addition to their writings, have given me valuable personal help and encouragement over the years for which I am deeply grateful. Louis Arnaud Reid, Professor Emeritus of the University of London Institute of Education, R. K. Elliott, also of the Institute, and Miss Ruby Meager of Birkbeck College, first enabled me to take a serious interest in philosophical aesthetics, and David Aspin, formerly of the University of Manchester, now Professor of Education at King's College, London, was a most sympathetic supervisor of my doctoral dissertation on parts of which I have drawn in this publication. I owe a very special debt to Dr. T. J. Diffey of the University of Sussex, who has been unremittingly kind and patient in reading and commenting in detail on various of my writings, including several chapters of the present volume. But my chief thanks go to Professor Eva Schaper of the University of Glasgow, who has similarly given me generous help and whose scholarship, especially in the field of aesthetics, together with her depth and breadth of understanding of the arts, have for a long time been a source of inspiration.

I am well aware, however, that not all the views expressed here are necessarily shared by these individuals, and any errors are, of course, mine alone.

H. B. Redfern
January, 1983.

CHAPTER ONE

Introduction

. . . the people most concerned with the arts are most antagonistic to the concern of philosophers with the arts.

Ruth Saw: *Aesthetics: An Introduction*

. . . it pays people interested in the arts and outside professional philosophy to look in regularly on aesthetics.

Joseph Margolis: *Philosophy Looks at the Arts*

During the twentieth century, developments in the dance as an art form have been on an unprecedented scale. Writing in 1946, A. V. Coton was not exaggerating when he said that

> the art of Theatrical Dance has undergone more sweeping changes of idiom and idea in the past thirty years than it experienced in the previous three hundred years (*The New Ballet: Kurt Jooss and His Work*, p. 11).

And since that time, of course, further significant changes, as well as changes in public attitudes towards the art of dance, have occurred.

Philosophical aesthetics, however, tends to remain somewhat preoccupied with the visual arts, with music, and with literature. Along with radio and television drama, the dance has not yet received from aestheticians the attention that might be thought commensurate with its popularity and cultural influence, although (as I shall discuss in Chapter 3), there would seem to be certain reasons for this which indicate serious deficiencies within the dance world as a whole.

Such neglect is apt to be felt especially keenly in those educational establish-ments in which there have been set up in recent years various kinds of degree courses in dance (sometimes in conjunction with other performing arts) that include aesthetics as a component of study. Whether this inclusion is sensible or realistic, particularly in the case of undergraduate courses, is questionable. For one thing there may be some truth in Plato's suggestion in the *Republic* (Book X) that an 'ancient quarrel' exists between philosophy and poetry – a suggestion endorsed by Ruth Saw in her remark quoted above. More importantly one might well fear for the quality of achievement that could be expected in such a notoriously problematic area. For aesthetics is a comparatively young discipline in which, as Eva Schaper points out, the scope for muddled thinking is wide indeed. It is often, as she puts it, 'the despair of clear-headed philosophers, and the delight of fringe-practitioners' (*Prelude to Aesthetics*, p. 9). Roger Scruton's

3

more recent reference to aesthetics as a 'continuing intellectual disaster' (*The Aesthetics of Architecture*, p. 292), while perhaps an over-pessimistic view, likewise indicates the stringent standards characteristic of philosophical enquiry.

Given therefore that considerable time is usually devoted to practical work in most dance courses, including those that typically precede post-graduate studies in the subject; that there is a deplorable lack of critical literature of any quality in respect of particular dance works; and that little is available for beginners in philosophy on aesthetics, the prospect seems daunting.

It is, of course, outside the scope of this book to consider questions such as to what extent the arts, conceived of as 'creative' or performing activities, as distinct from studies in their history, criticism, and appreciation, might be expected to flourish within an academic, or predominantly academic, environment; how practical aspects might be related to theoretical aspects; or at what sort of level (not to mention by whom) any creative endeavours might be assessed. Clearly, controversial issues far larger than either aesthetics or the arts are raised by the inaugurating of the sorts of courses in question[1]: what is ultimately at stake is nothing less than how the character and functions of a university, a polytechnic, or some other type of institution within the tertiary sector of education might be conceived. Nevertheless the situation regarding the study of aesthetics by those who have little previous training in philosophy is already with us and has to be faced.

Moreover it might be suggested that, in so far as a course is viewed as part of a *liberal* education, in contrast to an exclusively professional or technical training, the individual should be required to consider the nature of whatever activity in which he engages and not merely get on with the 'doing'.

Indeed in one important respect, despite what is popularly supposed, practice cannot be divorced from theory (using that term in a broad sense); for necessarily implicit within what a person does are certain beliefs and assumptions. These might be only vaguely formulated by the agent, if challenged, perhaps even barely recognised. But his aims and intentions, his very perception of what he is doing, presuppose conceptual frameworks that make it possible for him, in principle, to describe what is in hand and why he goes about it as he does. Now this, arguably, is not essential for an artist, *qua* artist; to have to examine his underlying presuppositions and make them explicit might be thought likely to inhibit, if not cripple, his creative efforts. A liberal education[2],

[1] For a most thoughtful and thought-provoking paper on the concept of a degree, what counts as academic study, and a number of other matters that are highly relevant to the question of degree courses in dance, see Best, D., 'A policy for the study of physical education and human movement'.

[2] For discussion of the concept of a liberal education that is relevant to this chapter, see Griffiths, A. P., 'A deduction of universities', and Hirst, P. H., 'Liberal education and the nature of knowledge'.

on the other hand, might be expected to equip an individual to reflect on his subject, to become acquainted with the various kinds of questions that might pertinently be asked in connection with it, and with the kinds of answers and verification procedures that are appropriate in each case (e.g. historical, scientific, moral), so that he comes to understand it within a larger perspective.

Furthermore it might be pointed out that many of those who are interested in the arts, not excluding artists and performers, often seem inclined from time to time to enter into what amounts to aesthetic discussion of sorts, even if only in an incidental and casual way (though usually without realising that what they are embarking on is a philosophical enterprise). They may, for instance, indulge in speculations about the nature of artistic meaning, form, expressiveness, imagination, whether certain qualities in an artwork or performance are 'really' there or not – let alone perenially controversial topics such as the nature of art or aesthetic experience. Yet in this they are perhaps no different from the majority of people. For example, the question 'What is art?', as T. J. Diffey observes in his paper, 'The idea of art', is apt to set individuals arguing far more readily and willingly in philosophy than topics such as causation or identity.

It is one thing, however, to ask a question that is in fact philosophical, quite another to recognise it as such, and further, to understand precisely what the problem is. It is yet a further task to wrestle with it with the sort of skill and persistence that philosophical investigation demands: in Socrates' famous phrase, *to follow the argument wherever it leads*. Anyone without the appropriate training is thus liable to flounder about in a mass of confusion – which is only compounded, it has to be admitted, by a good deal of literature (some calling itself 'philosophical') on the dance.

It is no doubt understandable that students should sometimes turn to the writings of artists and performers themselves – for example, the credos of the seven choreographer-dancers represented in Selma Jeanne Cohen's collection, *The Modern Dance: Seven Statements of Belief*. For the thoughts and experiences of those who dream and struggle and dare – and, more importantly, go on to achieve – are likely to have a particular appeal to anyone interested in composing and/or performing himself. Indeed it may be not only useful but essential to listen to what an artist has to say about his work, especially perhaps in the case of recent or contemporary art. On the other hand the situation is not always very different from that referred to by Plato:

> Well, gentlemen, I am ashamed to tell you the truth; but I must. Almost all the bystanders, with hardly an exception, one might say, had something better to say than the composers had about their own compositions (*The Apology*, 22A).

And when it comes to theorising about, say, dance or music or, more hazardous still, about art in general, practitioners in the arts, no less than anyone else lacking training in the kind of disciplined thinking required for high-level generalisation, are apt to go badly astray. Their 'statements of belief' – and they are rarely more than that – may even be conceptually naive, revealing little awareness, for example, of the dangers of trying to define certain words or of talking about *the* function or the *essence* of art (or dance, etc.). Moreover they tend to reflect passionately held, perhaps extreme, views and to be asserted in a categorical manner rather than argued for or defended rationally.

It is hardly to be expected that things should be otherwise. For to identify and elucidate problems to do with the nature of artistic meaning and communication, the relationship between artistic and everyday expression, the concept of art, and other similarly complex matters, is to be engaged not in art or art history or art criticism, but in philosophy. Where dramatists, choreographers, painters and so on 'speak' authoritatively is in their *works*, and these – their artistic 'statements' – are not to be confused with non-artistic remarks, whether of philosophers, critics, or artists themselves, *about* such 'statements'.

To make this distinction and, in the course of making it, to imply that an artwork is a sort of statement, yet not a genuine statement, is already to have embarked on a philosophical task. But before we pursue such a distinction, along with other aesthetic problems, it may be as well to anticipate the question: 'What *is* aesthetics?' Is it, for instance, as might appear from what has been said so far, concerned exclusively with art? And this question might, in turn, occur to readers alongside another: 'What sort, or sorts, of dance are here under consideration?' I shall devote the next chapter to the first question, but say something briefly now about the second.

Clearly, a great variety of forms and styles falls under the heading of 'dance'. Even within the relatively small compass of the United Kingdom there exists an enormous diversity, from folk dances whose origins and former significance are lost in the mists of time to 'folk' dances of our own day such as are found in ballrooms, dance halls and discothèques; from ancient ritual and ceremonial dances, such as the Sword and the Morris, to classical ballet and the modern dance of the theatre. There can then be a certain danger in making blanket references to so vast a subject. Yet since, as I try to show in later chapters, an aesthetic interest can extend – in principle, at least – to anything whatever, an account of such an interest does not require that it be specified in advance how a dance (say) might be classified.

This is not, however, to suggest that everything is equally likely to prove aesthetically rewarding; and throughout this book, for reasons that will emerge later, a good deal of discussion will centre on dance as a fine art. Precisely how this is to be delineated is far from easy or straightforward; but for the time being it may suffice to take as the art forms of dance those that involve works intended specifically for presentation to an audience, typically in a theatre or *quasi-theatre* setting, as contrasted with dance activities engaged in exclusively, or at any rate primarily, for social purposes or some further satisfaction of the participants. More detailed consideration of the concept of art will then be undertaken in Chapter 4.

CHAPTER TWO

What is aesthetics?

Like all philosophy, aesthetics is a process, not an end product, an inquiry, not an almanac. Probably the best way to put it is as old Socrates thought – it is a conversation among earnest minds.

Jerome Stolnitz: *Aesthetics*

Answers to the question 'What is aesthetics?' often begin by stating that it is a branch of philosophy. This, as it stands, is not quite accurate; and it can be misleading in two ways.

First, although the term 'aesthetics' used on its own usually does mean *philosophical aesthetics*, there are also *psychological aesthetics* and *sociological aesthetics*. Nevertheless before such empirical investigations can get under way at all, certain assumptions have to be made – about, for instance, what constitutes aesthetic interest, what counts as art. But a psychologist or sociologist does not always make explicit the position he adopts on such matters; he may in fact be unaware of exactly what that position is, what (logically) it commits him to, or how it differs from others that are possible. The philosopher, by contrast, part of whose job it is to scrutinise what is presupposed by the various categories of thought and awareness with which we operate, is concerned precisely to examine such assumptions, to probe underlying beliefs and attitudes, and to lay bare what usually remains tacit and unarticulated. Philosophical aesthetics is thus presupposed by, i.e., is logically prior to, empirical enquiries, and is in this sense of a more fundamental character; for unless it is clear what is being talked about, scientific investigations are pointless.

Secondly, to say that aesthetics is a branch of philosophy might seem to imply that it is a discrete area of enquiry, capable of being separated off from the rest of philosophy. Nothing could be further from the truth. Anyone who imagines that he can study philosophical aesthetics in isolation is hopelessly mistaken. For it is impossible to pursue aesthetic questions without encountering questions that are central to all philosophical enquiry – namely, questions of logic (in the broad sense of the study of principles of reasoning and valid argument); epistemology (the study of the nature, scope and sources of knowledge and of claims to know); metaphysics (the study of the structure of our thought about reality[1]); ethics; and, not least, philosophy of mind. This is to say that, far from

---

[1] This is an oversimplified statement. See further, for example, Winch, P., *The Idea of a Social Science*, especially section 1.

philosophy consisting of a number of independent strands, its various 'branches' are made up of clusters of problems sharing a common focus. The situation is thus quite different from that in, for example, the sciences, where it is possible to study, say, botany without also studying astronomy. While there are specialised areas of philosophical enquiry such as political philosophy, philosophy of law, of religion, art, education, and so forth, there are not, and cannot be, specialists in ethics or logic, for instance, but not epistemology or philosophy of mind.

It will be clear, therefore, that although a concern with art or education or science and so on might be what first prompts someone to become interested in philosophy and lead to a serious study of it, no amount of experience or expertise in that particular subject can provide *philosophical* understanding of it. However skilled or knowledgeable an individual might be in, say, one (or more) of the arts, he grapples when he asks aesthetic questions with problems of a sort fundamentally different from those he meets with in the course of composing, or performing, or critical appreciation. For philosophy is concerned with the nature and significance of knowledge that is already available: its questions are questions *about* other forms of activity and enquiry.

The philosopher of art then does not, *as* a philosopher, reflect on particular works or performances in the way that might lead him to say, as might a critic, that this dance is rather loosely structured but has moments of great beauty, or that Miss X gave a moving interpretation of such and such a role while Miss Y's was unimaginative and bordered on the sentimental. Rather, it is his job to examine the logical status of such claims, to distinguish them from remarks such as that a work is in rondo form or has three acts or that Miss Y substituted for Miss X last night; it is to contrast the kind of evidence that is appropriate in such differing cases; to unravel particular concepts (e.g., interpretation, sentimentality) and to trace their connections with others; to consider the relationship between, say, *Le Spectre de la Rose* (the work) and an instance of it (a particular performance); to ask whether a bad work is a work of art at all; and so on.

Since philosophy treats of questions to do with existing areas of knowledge, however, it might seem at first as if they are questions to be answered by experts within the area concerned. 'What is art?', for example, might appear to be a question for artists, or perhaps art critics or historians. But what is needed here is *conceptual* clarification; the enquiry is, in effect, a request for criteria by which one sort of thing may be marked off from another. Even if the question is rejected and an attempt made to show that it is one that should not be asked at all, at least not in that form, to discuss such a matter nevertheless remains a philosophical, not an artistic (or any other sort of) task. A good deal of misunderstanding persists on this point, and both the lay person and the specialist in a particular discipline are apt to fall into what D. J. O'Connor refers to as 'one of the commonest and most dangerous of intellectual errors – that of talking philosophy unawares' (*An Introduction to the Philosophy of Education*, p. 15).

A considerable amount of 'talking aesthetics unawares' may then go on among those closely involved with the arts. A choreographer, for instance, adopting a currently fashionable but completely mistaken view, may declare that what a dance means is just what anyone likes to make of it; a dancer may claim experience of aesthetic pleasure merely on the ground that his movements 'feel right', or even just 'feel good'; a teacher may believe that when children dance or paint they are essentially giving vent to emotional tensions. Individuals who would never presume to make pronouncements about the nature of, say, history or science or mathematics often jump in at the deep end when it comes to art. They do not hesitate, for instance, to expound on what art is 'basically about', or on the nature of the artistic process; to voice opinions on the *real* value of art in general or, say, the dance in particular; to insist that art (or dance, music, etc.) is a language – even, perhaps, that it is superior to verbal language; and, not least, to offer definitions of art, often quoting artists as 'authorities': 'Art is communication', '. . . the overflow of powerful feelings', '. . . the construction of forms', and such like (though all too often with little grasp of the thesis involved in each case or the background of thought against which it is to be understood).

To a certain extent this apparent readiness to plunge into what is philosophical debate has something to do with the nature of philosophy itself. For while some of the questions asked by philosophers may seem abstruse, even at times perverse, and while many *become* genuine questions for us only when someone with greater experience of philosophy obliges us to think afresh about things we normally take for granted, there are other questions of a philosophical kind that are liable to occur to anyone; and not only in his more deeply reflective moments, but in the course of dealing either with everyday affairs or with some specialised concern – for example, 'What is a dance?' As Diffey points out, there is a certain artificiality about the question 'What is a stone?' that is not the case with 'What is a poem?' We have to be argued *into* bewilderment about stones, he suggests, whereas we are immediately perplexed by the (note, grammatically similar) question about poems ('A place for works of art', p. 14).

Moreover everyone is already familiar to some degree with philosophical procedure. For, rather than consisting in special research techniques such as micro-processing or carbon-dating, it involves simply (though it is not, of course, always simple) an extension and refinement of our capacity to reason, and to analyse and construct arguments. What is gained in studying philosophy is the skill to do such things in a more systematic and more sophisticated manner, in particular by means of an increased sensitivity to questions of meaning and justification and a more precise handling of language. There would indeed, seem to be a good case for everyone having some training in philosophy.

Nevertheless there is no doubt that problems in aesthetics involve issues that are among some of the most profound and difficult in the whole of philosophy. For example, questions about meaning in the arts cannot be properly understood, let alone examined adequately, without an understanding of problems to do with meaning in general, which in turn involve complex questions about the relationship of language, thought, and perception to reality. It might be suggested in addition that philosophical enquiries to do with artistic and aesthetic issues are often aided by some knowledge of the history of art and art theory, as well as of aesthetics itself.

So far I have referred both to 'aesthetics' and to 'philosophy of art'. But the two are not synonymous; for aesthetics, at any rate in principle, extends to topics other than art. In practice, however, much contemporary aesthetic philosophy tends to concentrate almost exclusively on art and to become a kind of meta-criticism. Some philosophers have in fact implied that this is precisely what aesthetics is: the sub-title of Monroe Beardsley's *Aesthetics: Problems in the Philosophy of Criticism*, for example, makes the point explicitly. Yet such a view ignores a good deal of what would seem to be important objects of aesthetic interest – as, indeed, most philosophers (including Beardsley himself) acknowledge, even if they explore topics outside art only rarely. Aesthetic appreciation of nature, for instance, is such a subject. (For an unrivalled discussion of this, see R. W. Hepburn's paper.[1]) There are also activities such as folk dancing and ritual performances which, while not falling within the category of *fine art*, nevertheless often have aesthetic interest.

Moreover it is of some significance that aesthetics, evolving as it did only comparatively recently, namely in the middle of the eighteenth century ('that classical century of modern aesthetics', as it has been called[2]), originated specifically as a study of beauty, especially the beauty of nature. Historically, then, the concept of the aesthetic is grounded in the concept of the beautiful. The association of beauty with art, on the other hand, which also occurred in the eighteenth century, was a further development within the much longer history of art theory. But with the publication in 1746 of Charles Batteux' *Les Beaux Arts reduits à un même principe*, there was brought about a conjunction of the two ideas, beauty and art, that was to remain unchallenged for the best part of a hundred and fifty years, and that was so firmly established by the middle of the nineteenth century that 'fine' was often omitted from the term 'fine arts' ('beaux arts'): 'art' used on its own *meant* 'beautiful art'.[3] In searching for a principle by

[1] Originally published (and also reprinted) as 'Aesthetic appreciation of nature'; later in extended form as 'Contemporary aesthetics and the neglect of natural beauty'.

[2] Kristeller, P. O., 'The modern system of the arts', p. 108. This is a very useful text both on the arts and on aesthetics.

[3] Cf. Tatarkiewicz, W., 'What is art? The problem of definition today'.

which to distinguish activities such as painting, sculpture, poetry, music and the dance from others that we now classify as crafts or sciences, Batteux gave a fresh slant to the venerable idea of imitation: the fine arts, he proposed, sought to achieve the imitation of what was beautiful in nature. Thus the beauty of artworks was in effect conceived of as belonging to the wider category of natural beauty; and so it was also that philosophy of art became part of the study of beauty, or *aesthetics*.

Hence the otherwise puzzling name of this new area of enquiry. For what led the German philosopher Alexander Baumgarten to coin the term (or, rather, its German equivalent), adapting it from the Greek *aesthanesai*, to perceive, was his belief that beauty was a property of things when perceived as wholes. His book *Aesthetica* (published c. 1750) might therefore, in view of such a title, have been expected to deal with perception. Instead, though focusing almost exclusively on poetry and rhetoric, it attempted to provide a general theory of the arts in terms of the perception of beauty. And here it is possible to detect an early intimation of one of the most keenly contested issues in aesthetic philosophy during later years, namely the epistemological status of the aesthetic. For Baumgarten, while regarding aesthetic perception as involving knowledge, nevertheless attempted to identify it as something less than rational cognition, though something more than mere sensory awareness (see Schaper's *Studies in Kant's Aesthetics*, Chapter 5).

Indeed in the work of several German as well as British philosophers of the period, whose ideas paved the way for modern aesthetics *via* the most illustrious of them all, Immanuel Kant, we may recognize the seeds of what has become a fertile crop of problems that is still in the process of much winnowing and threshing. Such problems include not only those to do with beauty and other aesthetic qualities; with perception and the distinction between aesthetic and ordinary seeing and hearing; with ideas about 'sensuous surface' qualities, appearances and the looks of things; with cognition and the difference between aesthetic understanding and propositional knowledge (or 'knowing-that'); but also, since *aesthanesai* carries the additional connotation of direct awareness of feeling and emotion, problems centring on the nature of aesthetic experience as characterised in terms of pleasure, enjoyment or satisfaction (or their opposites).

Aesthetics then is of wider scope than philosophy of art. But is philosophy of art to be tied to aesthetics at all? This question, which would have been almost unthinkable prior to the second half of the present century (though challenges to the beauty/art connection by artists may be discerned much earlier), can best be understood against the background of developments in the arts since that time. For some recent forms have been explicitly *anti*-aesthetic, and their proponents argue that, although aesthetics is not now concerned exclusively, or even primarily, with questions to do with beauty, it nevertheless remains bound up with the idea of aesthetic experience. And this, they maintain, is irrelevant to art today: artworks are no longer designed for disinterested contemplation (a concept to be discussed in Chapter 7). Thus Timothy Binkley, for example, urges that

> philosophy of art must leave aesthetics in order to cope with art which is not fundamentally aesthetic, i.e., which does not choose to create with aesthetic qualities ('Deciding about art', p. 108).

It would seem important, therefore, to look in some detail at the concepts of art and the aesthetic and the relationship between them (see Chapters 4 and 5). However, it might be observed that it is often under the heading of *aesthetics* that this issue is itself discussed. Perhaps because of its over-riding concern now with art, aesthetics has extended beyond the idea not only of beauty, but also, paradoxically, of the aesthetic.

Two further points may be mentioned by way of concluding these brief remarks about philosophical aesthetics.

First, as may be evident from what has been said so far, the term 'aesthetics' (note the *s*) usually denotes a type of theoretical enquiry, while 'aesthetic' or 'the aesthetic' refers to the aesthetic mode of awareness itself. (Thus *discussions* about beauty, art, etc. – such as this volume – are not typically, though they could be, objects of aesthetic interest as, say, a ballet or a bouquet of flowers might be expected to be.) This is the practice I am following here; and I am taking aesthetics to embrace philosophy of art. It may be noted, however, that sometimes 'aesthetics' is used to denote aesthetic awareness, while (for example) 'Collingwood's aesthetic' is sometimes used in place of 'Collingwood's theory of art'. To add to the confusion, 'X's aesthetic' may be used in a very loose sense that has no significance whatever for philosophical enquiry to mean merely the credo or set of (unsystematised) beliefs of X about art – rather as 'philosophy' is used colloquially to refer to a few homespun opinions that X has about something or about life in general.

Secondly, it might be remarked that, like the larger question, 'What is philosophy?' the issue of precisely what aesthetics deals with always remains a matter for debate; and at present philosophical aesthetics is in a greater state of flux than at any other time in its (relatively short) history. Nevertheless, whatever differences of emphasis may occur, it will doubtless continue to share a feature of all philosophy that has persisted from its earliest beginnings, namely that of *dialectic* or conversation. Not, of course, conversation of a casual or trivial kind, but one in which the participants' concern is to pose questions, to suggest and pursue answers, to examine the nature of assertions of various kinds and the sort of evidence that might support or refute them, to draw out and develop the logical implications of what is stated or assumed, and to debate questions of value. Nor is this 'conversation' carried on only with other people. For in building up or following an argument one may talk, as it were, to oneself, putting forward or anticipating counter-arguments. Thus 'an objection to this might be . . . ', 'a further question that arises is . . . ', 'to this it might be replied . . . ' and so forth are not stylistic habits peculiar to a few writers, but ways of speaking (with variations, of course), that are fundamental to the philosophic enterprise. One seeks, that is, in aesthetics, as in all philosophical enquiry, to develop a critical listener/speaker within oneself.

This conversational character of the subject does not, however, mean that everyone's contribution is of equal merit, that there can be no progress in the area in question, or that it possesses no classics of its own. On the contrary, a somewhat unusual feature of philosophy is that much of its early literature remains not only of historical, but of continuing philosophical value and interest today. In authors such as Plato and Aristotle, for instance, we find aesthetic puzzles that are still the subject of considerable perplexity and that are, moreover, presented and debated in just such a way as to bring home the problem and stimulate further thought. *It is thus essential that even beginners in the subject should study primary texts at first hand.* To regard a book such as this, for example, as a substitute, would be a grave error.

Furthermore, in endeavouring to cultivate the habit of listening to what others have to say in a critical, yet open-minded manner, one has also to practise the discipline of writing and speaking lucidly oneself. A work of art may always strike us as something of a mystery; and the power of a great variety of things, events, performances and states of affairs to elicit an aesthetic response may also be a matter for wonder. But in *talk* about art, beauty, the aesthetic and related topics there is no place for mysteriousness or obscurity, for dogmatic assertion or vague speculation: what have to be striven for are clarity of exposition and soundness of argument.

CHAPTER THREE

The aesthetics of dance

No art suffers more misunderstanding, sentimental judgment, and mystical interpretation than the art of dance. Its critical literature, or worse yet its uncritical literature, pseudo-ethnological and pseudo-aesthetic, makes weary reading.

Susanne Langer: *Feeling and Form*

The sparsity of scholarly enquiry in the field of the dance, referred to in Langer's remarks of over a generation ago – which still, I submit, hold good in the main even today, in spite of her own efforts to improve matters[1] – prompts speculation as to possible reasons for this state of affairs. Is there some difficulty, or set of difficulties, in connection with the dance that is not shared by most of the other arts? Does the fault lie with philosophers, critics, choreographers, dancers, the dance-going public, or with all of these? In this chapter I offer some observations which, as well as trying to provide an answer to these questions, will raise incidentally certain issues that receive further consideration in later pages.

One reason for the neglect is historical. For despite the many facile claims that the dance is the oldest of the arts from which all the rest sprang (usually based on spurious arguments such as that the body is the immediate outlet for emotional expression), it has on the contrary tended to occupy an uneasy and in general rather lowly position among the fine arts; and it is on these, as noted earlier, that aestheticians mainly focus. Of course as a participant activity serving a great variety of functions – religious, social, didactic, and so on – the dance is of undoubted antiquity and significance. But as an independent art form intended for the enjoyment of an audience it has only comparatively recently begun to achieve any sort of maturity; and although Batteux identified the dance as one of his 'beaux arts', he nevertheless proceeded to treat it in conjunction with music, believing like many earlier theorists that the two essentially belonged together.

Moreover throughout the nineteenth century, relatively untouched by Romantic ideals of originality, creative imagination, and depth of feeling, the dance was somewhat out of line with the rest of the arts, neither its subject matter nor its formal features offering variety or profundity. Coupled with this – indeed, so it might be argued, largely responsible for it – there was no adequate

---

[1] For criticism of Langer's own work, see Macdonald, M., Review of *Feeling and Form*; Casey, J., *The Language of Criticism*, pp. 62–72; and Best, D., *Expression in Movement and the Arts*, pp. 184–189.

system of dance notation until well on into the twentieth century, though several ingenious experiments had been tried, some of which provided inspiration for later innovators; hence composition could not easily be separated from performance.

But better things might have been expected as regards aesthetic enquiry when, in our own century, more comprehensive forms of notation became available – notably, Kinetography Laban and the Benesh system – and when the dance began to struggle towards artistic autonomy. For with the development of modern dance in the United States and Central Europe there was more than a mere change of style: such a development constituted nothing less than a revolution in the conception of theatre dance. And here it is important to recall that in Europe, and in Germany in particular, choreographers, dancers and dance critics were well to the fore in that tremendous upsurge and flowering of artistic creativity in the years between the two world wars that is now widely regarded as having come close to matching the Renaissance of the sixteenth century, with a galaxy of extraordinarily gifted artists such as Thomas Mann, Herman Hesse, Berthold Brecht, Kurt Weill, Paul Hindemith, Arnold Schönberg, Paul Klee – to mention only a few. Not only was the dance, along with the other arts, often concerned with political, social and moral issues, but the continuing search for inspiration in the possibilities of bodily movement, the making of original accompaniments, including the use of the spoken word, the depersonalising of the dancing figure, the exploiting of technological devices and geometric design, together with much more that is today taken for granted but apt to be thought of as belonging to later times (and perhaps as distinctively American achievements), were already in full swing in Europe by the mid-1930s.

It seems doubtful, however, whether many aestheticians or art historians have been sufficiently aware of the radical nature of the changes that have come about in the dance in recent years. On the other hand, since philosophy of art is largely concerned with problems centring on the critical appreciation of artworks – problems of meaning, interpretation, evaluation, and so on – it has not, so to speak (as also in the case of radio and television drama), had a great deal to fasten onto. For criticism has not on the whole kept pace with developments in these art forms themselves. Thus, far from providing an understanding of dance works as kinetic constructs, most critics have continued to focus almost exclusively on the dancing and the dancers, and on such things as the set, costumes, accompaniment, story-line, and such like.

This is not to say that these are unworthy of comment, nor that in the performing arts enjoyment of presentation must detract from enjoyment of the composition. But there is always some danger that admiration of virtuosic performance may take precedence over appreciation of the work. It might indeed be suggested that in the dance world in general there is apt to be greater interest in dancing than in dances.

In this connection we should note further damaging effects of the lack of a universally accepted system of notation – perhaps, in fact, of there being two major systems currently in use. Not only is the corpus of dance works that has come down from the past but slight compared with the wealth of paintings, sculptures, musical scores, literary texts, and so forth; but there is no tradition of the careful study of dance scores for the purpose of seeking to understand compositions *as* compositions. A dancer might, of course, study a music score, but to suppose that in his dancing he is then interpreting either the music or that score would be absurd. Comparatively little therefore tends to be expected of dancers as interpretative artists in the way that we look to actors, pianists, conductors and the like for new insights into plays and musical works. (Consider the differences between master classes such as we see on television by great singers and instrumentalists as compared with those by dancers.) Hence there is far less opportunity for comparison and contrast and, with that, for changing response and appraisal in the case of a dance than with, say, a Schubert song-cycle or a Pinter play.

Some choreographer/dancers have in fact wanted their dances to die with them; and although the situation is now improving as regards new interpretations and reconstructions of dance works, the idea of *the* definitive performance seems to die rather hard in this realm. There are, of course, problems in the case of 'one-off', unrecorded performances; but, typically, any work of art not only permits but invites a variety of interpretations – and, further, seems to gain in stature as a result of this variety (one has only to think of *Hamlet* or Verdi's operas). As Margaret Macdonald once remarked, 'In art, the dead are never finally buried'.[1]

Nevertheless serious and sustained reflection on a dance is inevitably hindered by a feature of all movement, namely its transitoriness. Even when a script is available, and even supposing that the spectator is a competent reader, such a score cannot, as in the case of a music score, be followed simultaneously with a performance. There are also fewer chances for most people to see a dance many times, either 'live' or on film, than to listen, say, to recordings of music. But this would seem better regarded as a challenge to be met than as an insuperable difficulty; and while in practice not many people are as well acquainted with dances on the printed page as they are with musical works, the situation is in principle no different in the two cases.

Here once again, however, there seems to be considerable ignorance among philosophers and art historians. Harold Osborne, for example, states categorically that 'systems for the recording of ballet and dance have recently been devised, but they are still extremely esoteric and have far less precision

---

[1] 'Some distinctive features of arguments used in criticism of the arts', p. 125 (as reprinted in (ed.) W. Elton, *Aesthetics and Language*; page numbers throughout refer to this volume).

than literary and musical recordings'.[1] Yet it is difficult to see why Kinetography Laban – first made public in 1928, and now enjoying a world-wide reputation – should be considered any more esoteric or lacking in precision than the accepted form of music notation (I am unable to speak with sufficient knowledge about the Benesh system, but similar claims are made). In any case, the invention and use of symbol systems gives rise to questions of major philosophical interest – as witness, for instance, Nelson Goodman's *Languages of Art* (which devotes some space to the enterprise of recording movement).

It is, of course, no accident that Rudolf Laban's system was developed within the context of modern dance. For it is not geared to any particular style and does not presuppose knowledge of certain movements or positions, but is based on a detailed analysis of movement that makes it possible to record a variety of kinds. More than this, however, since it involves thinking in specifically kinetic terms, it can both serve as a compositional aid and assist in the appraisal of dance works by criteria peculiar to an art whose medium is bodily movement.

This is not to suggest that there may not be – there usually are – features of a dance that are interesting and valuable other than the handling of the movement material. Nor am I attempting to elevate formal criticism over, for instance, impressionist criticism: depending on the piece in question, there is surely room for a variety of approaches, one kind often complementing another[2]. There is also, clearly, a place for critical comment on particular presentations of a piece and for reports that convey something of what it was like to be 'there' on a particular occasion. Nevertheless there is a marked imbalance in much dance criticism, and it seems necessary to insist on the importance of giving due consideration, wherever appropriate, to the structural aspects of a work. For one of the chief functions of a critic, it might be agreed, is to enable others to understand artworks (Richard Wollheim suggests in his essay 'Criticism as retrieval' that in art discourse the word 'criticism' is used to make good a deficiency in the English language, namely a term for 'coming to understand': *Art and Its Objects*, p. 185). And although in all the arts, and especially in what has come to be called Post-Modern art, some items are, as it were, for instant consumption, self-consciously ephemeral, impermanent, others demand for their enjoyment an appreciation of their formal construction.

Compared with the achievements of, say, literary, film or music criticism, however, much of what passes for dance criticism is of a low-level, unscholarly kind. We just do not have detailed analyses of dance works by writers of the stature of, for example, Bernard Berenson, Donald Tovey, or I. A. Richards, or

[1] *The Art of Appreciation*, p. 169. Cf. also his more recent remarks in 'Aesthetic implications of conceptual art, happenings, etc.', p. 12.

[2] On different kinds of critical appraisal, see, for example, Stolnitz, J., *Aesthetics and the Philosophy of Art Criticism*, ch. 16.

– reaching a large lay public through their broadcasts – Antony Hopkins or Kenneth Clark. Moreover in addition to depth of understanding of one particular art form, what is often characteristic of a professional critic is knowledge of several arts. He is thus able not only to place a work or an artist within the correct historical perspective, but also to see it or him as having developed against a certain social and perhaps political background, and within a certain artistic and cultural tradition, even if – indeed, especially if – the artist concerned is in revolt against that tradition.

Most critics too are well acquainted with problems of the medium itself, perhaps with composing problems within the particular genre. We thus rightly take it for granted that, say, music critics have an appropriate technical vocabulary with which to refer to the internal relations and formal structure of a piece – otherwise they would be severely limited in their appraisal of a perform-ance *as* a particular rendering of the work in question (in philosophical language, as a 'token' of a 'type'[1]). Further, it is essential (as I discuss in more detail in Chapter 8), to be able to 'point' to, for instance, musical features such as perfect cadences or poetic devices such as sprung rhythm in order to try to justify an artistic appraisal. It is therefore unthinkable that a music critic should be unable to study a score at first hand and not be in the habit of returning to it constantly. Indeed it is doubtful whether music criticism and, in turn, musical aesthetics – *even, music itself* – would have developed and flourished as they have in the absence of a highly specialised vocabulary peculiar to the art, together with a sophisticated and widely used system of notation.

It might, however, be suggested that not a few dances in the theatre, as well as many outside, are of interest and value less for their complexity of structure and layers of meaning than for their *aesthetic* appeal in the narrow sense of that term – for their grace, elegance, and general harmony of movement; and that in such cases, as also in the case of much natural beauty, there may not be a great deal to be said by way of exegesis or critical comment. Certainly it would seem odd to try to point out what *makes* a dancer's movement graceful (or ugly, elegant, ungainly, etc.) to someone who failed to perceive such qualities.[2] Rather, we might wonder whether he understood these words; for it would seem precisely in the context of movement that they are likely to be learned and to have their central application (only derivatively do we speak of, for example, a graceful compliment, an elegant proof, a clumsy argument or a grotesque situation).

[1] Terms originally used to make a general philosophical point by C. S. Peirce (*Collected Papers, 1931–1935*). For a discussion related to aesthetics, see Wollheim, R., *Art and Its Objects*, pp. 79–84; and Charlton, W., *Aesthetics*, pp. 27–29, 32–33, 101–103.

[2] For further discussion on this point, see my 'Aesthetic qualities in the dance and their sig-nificance in education', pp. 216–241.

Nevertheless it does not follow that if there is little scope for analysis and critical discussion as regards elegant, harmonious movement, there is little of a controversial nature as regards harmonious, well-shaped dances. That is, artworks of any merit as *works*, and not merely as assemblages of movement that is pleasing to look at, require some measure of discriminating judgment – a capacity, we may note, that can be *educated*, typically with the assistance of someone well acquainted not only with the art form in question, but also with its discourse. Hence the need in each of the arts for a strong tradition of critical practice among both professionals and amateurs. Indeed without such a tradition there is some danger of an art failing to develop as fully as it might.

No matter what the box office returns, then, or the popularity of dance as a participant activity, its standing as a fine art is unlikely to rise as high as it might unless its critical literature is enlarged and enriched. Perhaps something depends on those for whom this book is primarily intended: *students* of the dance (in a wide sense of the term) who are, as such, prepared not only to give detailed attention to particular works, but also to engage in informed debate about those works, as well as to seek a better understanding of how the appreciation of art and of the aesthetic relates to, while differing from, other ways of structuring human experience. It may be that it is their reflections and questionings that will help to promote more enlightened criticism as well as further philosophical enquiry in this field.

CHAPTER FOUR

What is art?

Boswell: Sir, what is poetry?
Johnson: Why, Sir, it is much easier to say what it is not. We all *know* what light is; but it's
not easy to *tell* what it is.

James Boswell: *Life of Johnson*

It is not unusual, I suggested in the opening chapter, for those interested in the
arts – though not, so they may think, in philosophy – to ask nevertheless as a
result of that interest questions which are of an indisputably philosophical kind.
These are often of the form, 'What is . . . ?'; for example, 'What is rhythm?', '. . .
form?', '. . . dance?', and, not least, 'What is art?'

It may further be asked: 'Are ceremonial and ritual dances, such as the
Abbots Bromley Horn Dance, art? What about folk dances, American Square
dancing, ballroom and tap dancing? Is popular art a branch of art in general, or
not art at all?'

Or it might be said: 'Suppose someone creates a dance but never shows it to
anyone – is that art?' Comparable questions arise in respect of unpublished
poems, plays, novels, and such like, possibly lying undiscovered in a drawer
somewhere. Perhaps even more interesting, philosophically speaking, is an
undiscovered dance or music score; more problematic still, a song, a film scene,
etc. as yet 'in the composer's head' (Mozart is said to have carried whole
symphonies in this way). In other words, for something to count as art must it
be publicly accessible or can art be private?

Then what of talk of animals dancing? Zoologists sometimes speak, for
instance, of the courtship dance of the stickleback and the ritual dances of apes
(which so impressed Curt Sachs, who devoted the opening pages of his well-
known *World History of the Dance* to the reports of Wolfgang Köhler). Similarly,
what about birdsong, the singing of dolphins and whales, the products of a
chimpanzee supplied with paint, brushes and canvas, or of a monkey playing
with the keys of a typewriter?[1] Can there, that is, be animal art, or is art something created and presented only by human beings? Must there be the *intention*
to produce something to be seen as art?

What of objects found, say, on the beach (objets trouvés)? Can a piece of
driftwood, for example, be properly described as 'a lovely piece of sculpture'?[2]

[1] Cf. Collingwood, R. G., *The Principles of Art*, p. 126, fn.1.
[2] Cf. Weitz, M., 'The role of theory in aesthetics', p. 129 (as reprinted in (ed.) J. Margolis, *Philosophy Looks at the Arts*, second edition; page numbers will continue to refer to this publication).

How is it that soup tins, firebricks, and so-called Readymades such as a bicycle wheel or a urinal have been displayed – and apparently accepted – as art? Is it simply a matter of someone declaring certain things to be art?

Are 'happenings' in the theatre to rank as art? Or smoke sculptures and showers of sparks produced for no purpose other than to be looked at?[1] What of accidents – paint spilled on paper, notes or chords struck on, say, a piano or a guitar by mistake or at random, stumbles, falls, collisions, and other chance occurrences on the part of dancers? Are extemporised dance and music to rank as art, or must there always be some repeatable final form? Can something be an artwork if it is destroyed immediately after or even during the process of being made, or must it be capable of lasting through time? Is the term 'artwork' interchangeable with 'art', and does it imply excellence – or, to take the title of a paper by Cyril Barrett, 'Are bad works of art "works of art"?'

It must be said at once that I am not able, nor shall I even attempt, to deal fully with all these (and similar) questions. Rather, I shall seek to identify the major philosophical problems they raise that are currently, or have recently been, debated in aesthetics in connection with the question, 'What is art?', and hope that, on the basis of the discussion which follows (supplemented, of course, by further study), readers will be able to work out more specific answers for themselves.

It may be noted first that this question is apt to be construed as a request for a definition of the *term* 'art' – a definition, moreover, of the sort that seeks to sum up the *nature* or *essence* of the thing in question in terms of a certain characteristic or set of characteristics that make it just what it is and not something else. Clive Bell, for example, writing in 1915 and convinced that 'there is a peculiar emotion provoked by works of art', claimed that

> if we can discover some quality common to all and absent from none of the objects that provoke it, we shall have solved what I take to be the central problem of aesthetics. We shall have discovered the essential quality in a work of art, the quality that distinguishes works of art from all other classes of object (*Art*, p. 6).

Now if what is wanted here is a *verbal* definition that sets out both necessary and sufficient conditions for the correct application of the term – which is what many philosophers insist is the only sort of defining there is[2] – the request itself is of doubtful merit. For it suggests, as Wollheim[3] points out, that something

---

[1] Cf. Iwanska, A., 'Without art'.
[2] See, on this subject, Robinson, R., *Definitions*.
[3] 'Philosophy and the arts', p. 221.

can be said in a brief space that is adequate for the thing that is up for definition. The very form of the question, 'What is . . .?', tends to place constraints on the kind of answer that is sought: it is expected to be all-embracing, but concise. Yet to attempt this in the case of a phenomenon as complex and varied as art would seem an impossible task. As David Best has said, 'the demand for a definition is often in effect a demand for distorting oversimplicity' (*Philosophy and Human Movement, p. 19*).

Even within a limited period and within the same culture the manifestations of what is commonly regarded as art are extraordinarily diverse, ranging from literature to sculpture, from music to painting, from architecture to the dance, etc. – not to mention the variety of their genres (e.g., epic poems, picaresque novels, jazz ballet). Like 'beauty', 'aesthetic appreciation', 'form', and many other terms, 'art' would seem to be precisely the kind that resists satisfactory definition in neat epigrammatic form – although examples of just such formulae abound: 'Art is expression of emotion', '. . . is significant form', '. . . is objectified subjectivity', and so on.

The problem is not, however, simply one of brevity, of the inappropriateness of a few words on a vast subject. Rather, the question is whether 'art' is the kind of term that can be defined (in the strict sense) at all. It has certainly been the view of many philosophers who have adopted an approach to the subject in the spirit of Ludwig Wittgenstein – the later Wittgenstein, one should say[1] – that it cannot; that the task is not merely *as a matter of fact* difficult, but logically impossible. The traditional quest for answers to 'What is art?', 'What is beauty?', and the like, has therefore been widely rejected as a proper subject for philosophical enquiry during the second half of this century. Such questions, it has been insisted, are unreal questions, logically misbegotten; to ask them is to misunderstand the kind of idea or concept under review. No condition can be found necessary, let alone sufficient; generalisations can only be vapid or, if intelligible at all, either trivially true (and so, uninformative) or so contentious as to be scarcely of any value, merely indicative of the preferences of certain people at a certain time in a certain milieu.

Weitz' influential paper 'The role of theory in aesthetics' (first published in 1956) epitomises this viewpoint. Traditional theories of art, he claimed ('theory' being used here in a special sense to denote enquiry into the nature of something such that it yields necessary and sufficient conditions for the correct application of the term in question), not only are liable to prove circular, incomplete, untestable, pseudo-factual, and so forth, but are logically vain attempts to define what is undefinable; further, to lay down a set of defining properties of

---

[1] It is customary to speak of the 'earlier' and the 'later' Wittgenstein to mark the change in his view of language and, with that, of the nature of philosophy, that occurred between the writing of his *Tractatus Logico-Philosophicus* (published in 1921) and his *Philosophical Investigations* (published posthumously in 1953).

art would seal it off against development, would foreclose on creativity. Because of what Weitz refers to as the 'very expansive, adventurous character of art, its ever-present changes and novel creations', the conditions for the correct application of the term 'art' can never be exhaustively enumerated (p.127). (It may be noted, however, that Weitz does not hestitate here to mention what sound like certain necessary features of art.) Traditional theories nevertheless often have the virtue, he urges, of pinpointing aspects of art that are worthy of attention yet may have been neglected or distorted by previous accounts. As William Kennick put it in another famous paper of the 1950s, 'as definitions they will not do; but as instruments of instruction or reform they will do'.[1] Such formulae, that is, serve as slogans for changing taste, as a means of refocusing attention and opening up new avenues of appreciation. It is hardly surprising then, as Kennick goes on to remark, that they have had more weight with critics than with philosophers. Thus Clive Bell and Roger Fry, for instance, eager to challenge Edwardian preferences for painting of the figurative kind, sought with their definition 'art is significant form' to promote an entirely new conception of art, namely as involving a particular sort of response to the *formal* features of artworks – qualities of line, colour, shape (in the non-visual arts, features such as melody, rhythm, harmonic progression).

Some of these definitions, often advanced with the express intention of revising the existing idea of art, might indeed be regarded as instances of what C. L. Stevenson labelled 'persuasive definitions' – formulae that endow a word which has strongly emotive overtones with a particular meaning that the author, often speaking with an authoritative ring, tries to get others to accept as the 'real' or 'true' meaning – terms which themselves, Stevenson suggests, typically indicate the nature of the definition being offered ('Persuasive definitions', p. 334).

This might lead us to reflect further on the purposes of traditional accounts of art. For what many, if not most, would seem to have been principally concerned with is the excellence of artworks, and with what makes for that excellence: in Weitz' phrase, they are 'honorific definitions' as contrasted, he claims, with descriptive uses of the term 'art'. What was said on behalf of art in general was thus said on behalf of examples of merit: the possibility of bad art was not considered – perhaps implicitly ruled out. It might therefore be doubted, as Diffey suggests in his paper 'Essentialism and the definition of art', whether in fact earlier writers on art were seeking primarily to get to grips with *meaning*. For it is possible to distinguish questions about a set of criteria for determining what is a work of art from enquiries about the nature of the category of art. A related point is made by Wollheim:

---

[1] 'Does traditional aesthetics rest on a mistake?', p. 10 (as reprinted in (ed.) C. Barrett, *Collected Papers on Aesthetics*; page numbers will continue to refer to this publication).

There is an important difference between asking what Art is, and asking what (if anything) is common to the different kinds of work of art or different arts (*Art and Its Objects*, p. 4).

Although we may not be able to provide a strict definition of a term then, it does not follow that nothing can be said about the character of whatever is under discussion; and some theories of art that have been most under attack, Diffey suggests, might be viewed as having aims to do not so much with meaning as with knowledge. What they were attempting was to explain what sort of phenomenon art is – for example, to make a case for the idea that art is a kind of play.[1]

Certainly it would be a serious mistake to suppose that most of those writers whose work issued in what appear to be pithy definitions (such as those instanced earlier) merely made sweeping pronouncements in the form of memorable aphorisms. On the contrary such compact statements are usually no more than shorthand summaries of what are substantial theses. Moreover, while some theorists did exclude all but one aspect of art – that which they insisted was of supreme importance – they were less 'one-idea'd', so observed W. B. Gallie (an early critic of the 'essentialist fallacy'[2]), than the labels attaching to their theories might suggest. 'Time and again', he wrote, in another celebrated paper of the 1950s, 'Art as an essentially contested concept',

we find them letting in, as it were anonymously and by the back door, 'subordinate considerations' . . . which their formal definitions exclude, but without reference to which their theories would be patently one-sided and [*sic*] unplausible (p. 113, fn.).

The initial inspiration for traditional aesthetic theories of the essentialist kind, Gallie further claimed, often came not from men who were primarily philosophers, but from 'men of great insight into two or more of the arts and very forceful exponents of some new movements of feeling and aspiration in the critical appreciation of the arts' (p. 102). The extent to which traditional theories of art may still affect professional art criticism, as well as the responses of lay people, should not indeed be underestimated. However rarely they may read philosophical or critical literature of earlier times, what has been said about art, especially when vividly expressed, often continues to influence looking, listening and reading today. Thus traces of doctrine derived from, for example, Wordsworth, Coleridge, Tolstoy, Arnold, Hegel, Collingwood, are

---

[1] On this idea, see, for instance, Schiller, J. F. C., *On the Aesthetic Education of Man*; and Huizinga, J., *Homo Ludens*.

[2] See his 'The function of philosophical aesthetics' (first published in 1948).

often deeply ingrained in people, even if they are unaware either of the origins or the wider implications of those ideas.

Of course speculation and discussion about art and works of art differ considerably in their aims and range over a wide variety of topics; and Diffey may well be right that 'anti-essentialists' such as Kennick and Weitz *stipulated* which theories were to count as traditional – or else themselves fell into the essentialist trap of supposing that all such theories shared a common viewpoint. But whether or not these mid-century philosophers and their followers were correct about the main concerns and intentions of their predecessors, the search for a satisfactory account of art persists. We might then consider what those philosophers critical of traditional theorists have themselves had to say by way of a more positive approach.

Two major recommendations have been proposed along Wittgensteinian lines (though Wittgenstein himself did not apply them specifically to the concept of art). First, that instead of asking 'What does "art" (or "work of art") mean?' we should consider how the word or phrase is commonly used and accepted in everyday language. This, Weitz (for example) confidently asserts, 'is the initial question, the begin-all if not the end-all of any philosophical problem and solution' (p.125). The task is to give a logical description of the functioning of a concept, what it *does* in the language; or, as Gallie puts it, 'the answer is always already there *in the words as properly used*' (p. 98).

Secondly, instead of trying to discover some property or properties common and peculiar to the various instances of (say) art, we should look for *family resemblances*. The model here is Wittgenstein's well-known advice in respect of a game:

> Don't say: 'There *must* be something common or they would not be called 'games' – but *look and see* whether there is anything common to all (*Philosophical Investigations*, para. 312).

What we shall find, rather, is 'a complicated network of similarities overlapping and crisscrossing'; in *The Blue and the Brown Books* the metaphor is that of a rope held together by a vast number of fibres, even though no single fibre runs from one end to the other (p. 87).

To take the first suggestion then: a highly abstract term such as 'art' or 'beauty', unlike 'table' or 'tree', for instance, has a plurality of uses, a complex – though not, as Kennick insists, mysterious – logic. This, of course, is evident from any dictionary, which gives a list of various meanings of a word: 'skill', 'guile', 'craft', 'painting'; etc. in the case of 'art'. But a dictionary does not tell us what we usually want to know when we ask, 'What is art?' This, it is maintained on an 'ordinary language' approach, can only be *shown* or *displayed* by examining how the word or phrase in question, along with its correlates and derivatives, is used in a range of familiar contexts, and by comparing and contrasting those uses not only with one another but with those of other abstract terms that are relevantly similar.

This recommendation often at first strikes the enquirer as rather disappointing and unsatisfactory, however; for there would seem to be a danger of going round in circles. Having spotted that there is talk of 'correct' or 'proper' uses, we might well think that this is begging the whole question. What *are* these correct uses, and how are we to recognise them? Equally to the point, what are *in*correct uses? If, for example, *you* refer to tap dancing (or a game of football, birdsong, or a firework display) as art and I challenge you on this, are we just using the same word in different ways (i.e., misunderstanding which *sense* of the term is being employed), or do we agree about the sense but disagree about what we believe to be its correct application (i.e., about the *reference*)? In the first case we can easily sort out our misunderstanding: 'Ah, I see – *you* are talking of skill, a high level of precision, cleverness and so on in the execution of certain rhythms, patterns, etc. *I* was thinking of something more: skill, certainly (something that can, incidentally, be taught, practised, improved upon), but also involving imagination, originality, feeling (something that perhaps cannot be taught directly)'. (This, it must be stressed, is purely hypothetical, for purposes of illustration.) In the second case, however, there are likely to be more serious differences to be resolved. For you might retort: 'But that's what tap-dancing (say) does involve – it does involve imagination, originality, feeling . . . It *is* art!'. 'But what's imaginative about it?', I might then reply. 'What do you mean here by "imagination", "originality" (etc.)?' The debate would therefore call for further examination of the way in which we are each using these terms in this particular context – precisely what the 'appeal to ordinary language' advocates.

In this way we are turned aside from looking for any common denominator shared by tap-dancing, football, birdsong, and so on; and, far from any doubts as to what is correct or incorrect usage constituting a defect or weakness of such an approach, this, it is urged, is a positive advantage. For we are obliged to think more carefully about how we do use certain terms, to try to state more succinctly which sense we have in mind, to put forward reasons for or against a particular usage in a particular case. And in striving to make clear what we mean, and thereby to achieve better understanding and communication with others, we shall probably soon find that we do, indeed, begin to draw parallels, to make distinctions, to notice interesting and significant differences and similarities. We are likely, too, in gaining a clearer idea of other people's conceptions of art, to become more precisely aware of what our own consists in, and to see what other perspectives we have (*must* have) in order to maintain this perspective consistently; we might even come to modify or change it altogether.

Nevertheless Kennick's claim that 'we are able to separate those objects which are works of art from those which are not, because we know English' (p. 6), may leave us with certain nagging doubts – especially as regards the 'we' he refers to. For if, as he suggests, someone instructed to bring out all the works of art from a warehouse containing a great assortment of objects (e.g. pictures, vases, tools, boats, books, postage stamps) can do so 'with reasonable success', a good deal might be thought to depend on who and what are involved. Diffey poses some pertinent questions:

> Who, for example, is undergoing the test – a weekend painter, a politician, the man on the Clapham omnibus, the President of the Royal Academy, a student in the Academy school? Whose work is in there among the machines, the furniture, etc? Who determines that the test has been passed? Shall we allow Tolstoy to adjudicate, or Pater or Mrs. Grundy? ('Essentialism and the definition of art', p. 112).

(There is also the further problem of the dance scores, which it is interesting to note Kennick includes in his list, even though he speaks of them as 'musical scores . . . for dances' – a problem that is part of the larger question, also mentioned by Diffey, whether a work of art is, or in some way is, a physical object.[1])

A participant in the 'warehouse test' then, Diffey argues, may rightly hesitate about whether to bring out all the poems, pictures, etc. or only those he considers deserve the label 'art'. On the one hand there is the well-established point that we often understand the meaning of a word without being able to define it: Kennick, like Wittgenstein, cites the famous reply of St. Augustine to the question 'What is Time?' – 'If I am not asked, I know; if I am asked, I know not'. Yet against Kennick's stronger claim that a definition is a positive hindrance to an understanding of 'art', Diffey puts forward the counter-paradox that the more someone knows and cares for art, the less competently (according to Kennick's criteria) he will perform the test. For someone's grasp of the concept of art can hardly be unaffected by whatever knowledge of and interest in works of art he has (or lacks); and it is surely unacceptable that those who know and care least for art should appear to have the better understanding of the word 'art'. Kennick must therefore be using it in a classificatory, not an evaluative sense, Diffey concludes.

Such a distinction is far from clear cut, however; and certainly Weitz is hardly convincing when he tries to illustrate the classificatory (or descriptive) sense of 'art', since he speaks of 'some sort of artifact, made by human skill,

---

[1] For discussion of this, see Wollheim, R., *Art and Its Objects*.

ingenuity, and imagination' – criteria that are clearly not without evaluative overtones. They rule out, as Barrett[1] observes, the utterly trite and banal, for instance, as well a good many other unadmirable attributes. Moreover, as we saw earlier, Weitz also ascribes expansiveness, adventurousness, and originality to art, features that again are usually regarded favourably rather than in a neutral way. It in fact proves more difficult than might at first be supposed to make a satisfactory case for neutral or non-evaluative uses of the terms 'art' and 'work of art' – indeed the idea of a neutral description of anything at all is perhaps a chimaera. The best we can do, it would seem, is to distinguish between *more* and *less* evaluative uses, the latter letting in, in the case of art, the possibility of mediocre or indifferent – if not actually bad – instances.

Furthermore Kennick introduces an additional difficulty when he claims that, whereas someone sent to fetch an object possessing 'significant form' or all the objects of 'expression' would have little or no idea of what to look for, he nevertheless knows a work of art *when he sees one* (my italics). This is a problem that leads us to consider the second move that has proved attractive to those opposing essentialism in art, namely that invoking the idea of family resemblances. For Kennick's remark raises the crucial question (which he leaves undiscussed, however), of what *sort* of seeing is involved in connection with art.

We might begin by noting a serious criticism that is often levelled at the family resemblances model in general.[2] In the case of an actual family such as the Hapsburgs or the Mitfords, one of whose members might resemble another in respect of the nose, another the lower lip, another the chin – or the hair, gait, and so on – we already have the family determined for us. These traits are family likenesses because the individuals concerned belong together in the first place by virtue of genetic ties: if someone not related by blood happened to look like a Hapsburg or a Mitford he or she could not be said to bear a *family* resemblance. But in the case of artworks, as well as many other things to which the model has been applied, how are we to identify the individuals between which likenesses are to be traced? What corresponds, that is, to the genetic tie? However if we knew this, we might want to say, the puzzle as to what is to count as art would not have arisen in the first place. We thus seem to be left with the precise problem that the notion of family resemblances was called in to solve.

One answer might be that we have to start with central cases which would seem indisputably to be art and then work outwards, so to speak. If, for example, *King Lear*, *War and Peace*, *Giselle*, *The Birth of Venus*, *The Magic Flute*, *Citizen Kane*, *Lycidas*, *The Green Table*, the *Eroica* symphony and so on are not art,

[1] 'Are bad works of art "works of art"?', p. 186.
[2] See, for example, Mandelbaum, M., 'Family relationships and generalisations concerning the arts'.

what is? We seek, that is to say, relevant similarities between such cases as these and other particular cases. As with a moral question where we might look for an analogous instance of which we are prepared to say, 'Well, surely *that* was the right (or wrong) thing to do', we can try to find recognisably similar instances in the case of artworks. (Indeed, a common way of enquiring about the nature of a thing or person is to ask what it or he or she is *like*.)

But now we meet the problem of what is to count as relevant. For of course not any kind of similarity will do; the nature of the resemblance has to be of significance. Hence another general objection to the idea of family resemblances in this connection – that, given a little ingenuity, we could find likenesses between almost *any* two things. It is hardly helpful to point out, say, that all artworks involve the displacement of air or are the subject of numerous books. It might have been expected, then, that it would be just this challenge that would have been taken up by those who have turned with such alacrity to the idea of family relationships as applied to art – that diligent attempts would have been made to work out with some precision what the supposed network of relationships consists of, what sorts of strands of similarities count as relevant, and such like. But such expectations have not been fulfilled. Gallie, originally sympathetic to the idea (as evident in his paper 'The function of philosophical aesthetics'), later expressed doubt as to its usefulness; for it offers, he maintains,

> no explanation of why, among all the conceivable sets of overlapping resemblance that could be traced between and among, say, printed books, vocal performances, rhythmic bodily movements and pictorial representations, *one particular line of resemblances*, or one set of such lines, has been picked out and valued under the rubric 'work of art' ('Art as an essentially contested concept', p. 101).

Maurice Mandelbaum would therefore seem to be right in seeing the notion of family resemblances as having been used only negatively in respect of art.

Yet if such a set *were* to be worked out this would ultimately impose unacceptable limitations. It might be possible in principle – though in practice the task would be of overwhelming magnitude – to trace significant similarities among the vast body of items already acknowledged as artworks. But the exercise would be pointless; for even as we did so, some artist (especially a well-established artist) could come along with a new 'offering' which would cast doubt on, if not completely ruin, any such scheme. This is not to say that *no* important similarity or similarities – as well as important dissimilarities – could be found between the new arrival and the rest; indeed, if it were otherwise, as I shall discuss further in a moment, there would be no reason to see it as art at all. But a particular *set* of resemblances laid down here and now, or at any other point in time, would be likely to exclude later candidates. In fact the only sort of occasion when it is profitable, and indeed necessary, to trace connections between artworks is when doubt does arise (say, among Customs officials) as to whether something so astonishingly different from what has previously been accepted as art, but is now presented as such, *is* to count. This is one of the few circumstances in which a *decision* is called for as to what is art and what is not.

One aspect of the problem of resemblances which certainly requires elucidation has to do with the qualities or properties that are to be compared. For the terms 'qualities', 'properties', 'features' and such like are apt to give rise to a major problem, namely what is available to ordinary perception. For instance several critics of traditional theories of art would seem to have supposed that what the authors of those theories had in mind when they spoke in 'essence' terms were qualities or properties of a directly observable kind – or what they thought was directly observable. Perhaps in some cases this was so, especially among those of a formalist persuasion, whose accounts do sometimes sound as if, for example, form, beauty, unity, harmony are actually *there* to be seen *in* the work. Yet such qualities have rarely been considered discernible in the way that features such as redness, hardness or circularity are thought of as discernible; moreover many traditional accounts of art focused not so much on artworks themselves as on, say, the (alleged) effect of art on the percipient (e.g., a special kind of pleasure); or on what was thought to be the creative artist's activity or mental state (e.g., the expressing of emotion); or on the relationship between the artist and his public (e.g., a bond of union between man and man).

When Wittgenstein invites us to *look and see* what strands of similarities exist between various instances of (e.g.) art, it is indeed conceivable that this is not to be taken literally. Rather, what might be more significant are not directly manifested, but non-exhibited characteristics, as Mandelbaum suggests. Similarities and relationships between various objects, performances, etc. might, for example, be established in respect of origin, function, intention or purpose (though Mandelbaum himself does not try to make a case for any of these in the case of art). In a much later paper, and from a very different perspective, as mentioned in the previous chapter, Binkley almost echoes Mandelbaum on this point: 'Properties of objects', he says, 'are fundamentally irrelevant to art status . . . . Arthood is a relation, not a property' ('Deciding about art', p. 97).

The claim that what distinguishes art is not anything immediately available to direct visual or auditory inspection is of first importance, and has been taken up and elaborated by a number of philosophers. It seems to have been voiced first in an explicit manner by Arthur Danto in a controversial paper of 1964, 'The artworld', in which he argued that to see something as art 'requires something the eye cannot de[s]cry – an atmosphere of artistic theory, a knowledge of the history of art: an artworld'.[1] We cannot, for instance, know that a dance is a work of art just by examining the movements involved (indeed we cannot even know that it is a dance[2]). Rather, artworks are to be distinguished by their central role in a whole complex of social activities and practices that includes creating and producing, performing and presenting, criticising and reviewing, marketing and financing, and so forth. The problem, of course, is how to provide a sufficiently precise characterisation of such activities and practices so that they pertain specifically to art and not to other things as well. For a great variety of items that are *not* art are created, presented, appraised and so on – even in places such as theatres, museums, galleries, concert halls, libraries, and the like, which typically do house artworks. Nevertheless the recognition of art as a social and historical phenomenon, quite unlike, say, sun, darkness, cold or stickiness, would seem vital for any satisfactory analysis of the concept.

While Danto's idea of an 'artworld' was new to aesthetic enquiry, however, it owed a good deal to the insight, deriving largely from Wittgenstein, that in order to understand a vast host of concepts, of which art is a notable example, it is essential to have a grasp, to be on the inside, of what Wittgenstein variously referred to in his *Lectures and Conversations on Aesthetics* as 'a whole culture', 'the whole environment', 'ways of living', or, in the *Philosophical Investigations*, 'a form of life'.[3] To see something as a work of art then is not to recognise a 'brute fact', but depends on what can be known or taken for granted about the *context* (Danto's 'atmosphere') of the object in question; and that context is of an institutional kind. As with, for instance, supplying someone with potatoes[4] or booking a ticket for a theatre – which may seem very ordinary occurrences, yet in fact involve an intricate web of assumptions and beliefs that normally are not made explicit – so the knowledge needed to regard something as an artwork and to appreciate it *as* art requires acquaintance with the institutional framework in which such practices and activities are embedded.

Thus we are able, for example, to understand a set of bodily movements in terms of the art of dance and not (whatever outward similarities there may be) of, say, a magic ritual, a gymnastic display, or a set of therapeutic or physical fitness exercises, because we belong to a society in which, typically, one group – the audience – watches, and may pay money to watch, another group or an individual give a performance in a special space such as a theatre or *quasi-theatre* (e.g. a park, a school hall), where the proceedings are regulated by certain conventions. These conventions may, of course, be modified to a greater

---

[1] See p. 16, as reprinted in (ed.) Aagaard-Mogensen, L., *Culture and Art*; page numbers refer to this publication.

[2] Cf. Best, D., *Expression in Movement and the Arts*, pp. 36–37.

[3] For a discussion of his varying uses of this term, however, see Hunter, J. F. M., ' "Forms of life" in Wittgenstein's *Philosophical Investigations*'.

[4] Cf. Anscombe, G. E. M., 'On brute facts'.

or lesser extent: audiences may be invited to participate themselves in some way; stages, lighting and special costumes may be dispensed with; a street may become, temporarily, 'the boards'. But no matter how experimental or revolutionary the presentation, either in terms of *what* is presented or *how*, there have to be sufficient likenesses between the old and the new frameworks for us to be able to accommodate any innovations within our existing concept of art. When we question whether something is a new form of art or not art at all, it is precisely when the institutional framework is strained to breaking point – as, for instance, when an audience is required to explore a maze in a loft, finally discovering (or not, as the case may be), a dancer lying motionless, and the whole 'performance' is claimed to be a dance.[1] But as long as a few conventions remain it is possible that our concept of art, or of a particular art form, is expanded and enriched, perhaps drastically revised.

So-called Institutional theories of art then have been much canvassed in recent years. Indeed George Dickie, one of the foremost proponents of such a theory, formulated in the late 1960s a would-be definition of the strict kind along these lines, thus attempting what had by then come to be widely regarded as an outdated and futile task. This definition, first put forward in a paper, 'Defining art', he has since elaborated and defended in a number of publications, taking as a starting point Danto's idea of an artworld (not so far developed any further by Danto himself), and eventually producing the formula:

A work of art in the classificatory sense is 1) an artifact 2) a set of the aspects of which has had conferred upon it the status of candidate for appreciation by some person or persons acting on behalf of a certain social institution (the artworld) ('What is art?' p. 23).

Predictably this definition bristles with problems, which have duly been sifted and debated by numerous critics. There is the question, for example, of what is to count as an artifact, what 'conferring' amounts to here, what sort of appreciation Dickie is concerned with (the very term raising doubts about the propriety of his claim to be defining art in a classificatory sense). These issues will enter into the ensuing discussion, even if somewhat indirectly, as we proceed; but first we may consider some further questions about the central notion here, that of the artworld.

Who, for instance, is to be regarded as a member of it, and how is this brought about? Dickie, anxious to avoid any restrictions that would operate against freedom and creativity in art, and insisting that by 'institution' he means established practice, not an established society or corporation, claims

[1] Cf. Banes, S., *Terpsichore in Sneakers*, p. 189.

that 'every person who sees himself as a member of the artworld is an "officer" of it and is thereby capable of conferring status in its name' (*Aesthetics: An Introduction*, p. 104). But in that case, where does one draw the line? For it would seem from this that anyone could pronounce anything a work of art, or at least a candidate for appreciation (whatever might be meant by that). Since membership could, in principle, be extended to everyone, the result would be that the artworld would be co-extensive with society as a whole and so lose any identity it might be thought to have; the whole notion then becomes redundant. Moreover Danto's original point about art needing 'an atmosphere of artistic theory, a knowledge of the history of art' certainly rules out some, perhaps most, people. On the other hand the suggestion of an élite of some kind runs into the difficulty of perhaps rendering the artworld either so conservative or so radical as to restrict unjustifiably what may count as art.

An adequate characterisation of the artworld requires therefore that somehow a course be steered between completely undifferentiated membership at one extreme and élitism at the other. This Diffey attempts in his paper, 'The Republic of Art', which, interestingly enough, appeared at almost the same time that Dickie launched *his* theory of art, and was expressed, at least in part, in strikingly similar terms. Not surprisingly, somewhat similar problems are encountered. In contrast to Dickie, however, Diffey takes art to be an inescapably evaluative concept; the notion of a Republic of Art, like the eighteenth-century idea of a Republic or Commonwealth of Letters, from which it is adapted, implies reference to authority of some kind. For there is a difference, Diffey rightly insists, between some person *saying* that something is a work of art and its *being* one: it has to be accepted as such by other people, not merely offered. The situation is similar, he suggests, to certain other institutional practices such as the awarding of degrees by a university (though the analogy cannot be pressed very far).

Nevertheless there is the question of the fallibility of this hypothetical Republic (or, indeed, of any proposed artworld). As with the awarding of degrees, Diffey points out, mistakes are sometimes made: it can happen that undeserving candidates are honoured, while others who merit acclaim are rejected or passed over and so go unrecognised, at least for a time. (We might recall here, for instance, the hostile reception of Martha Graham's dances in this country in the 1950s.) But whilst errors do occur from time to time, it does not follow that what counts as art is not, ultimately, a public matter.

This, indeed, is one of the most valuable points insisted on by writers who draw attention to the institutional character of art. Just as there cannot be a private language,[1] it is argued (following Wittgenstein), so is art essentially public. What is art cannot be determined according to personal whim or even

---

[1] See, for example, Rhees, R., 'Can there be a private language?'.

the serious reflective judgment of a single individual. As with moral questions, nobody can set himself up as a solitary arbiter in respect either of his own 'works' or anyone else's – which is not, of course, to say that revolutionaries do not bring about change in the realms of both conduct and art, merely that no individual can ever be entirely independent of the standards of the culture to which he belongs. The most 'free-thinking' radical *is* radical only in the light of what is generally accepted; revolutionaries and innovators have to be familiar with certain norms in order to revolt against them. What is needed to serve as justification in doubtful cases of art, therefore, as Diffey rightly saw at the beginning of the 'institutional' debate, is *argument*, or perhaps some sort of explanation of what the artist (if such he is) seems to be doing.

This point has been developed by Wollheim in a recent essay on the institutional theory of art,[2] in which he maintains that the crucial question to be asked of definitions such as Dickie's, which speak of conferring art status on some artifact, is whether this is done *for good reasons*. If there are such reasons. Wollheim argues, then not only should this be made clear in the definition, but some account should be given of what makes them good. In that case, however, art status is *recognised* or *confirmed* rather than conferred, since the artifact must enjoy this status prior to any conferring action: this part of the definition is thus inessential. If, on the other hand, there are no reasons, or the reasons are bad, the whole idea seems very odd; for why then should any importance be attached to the 'candidate for appreciation'? Unless the 'person acting on behalf of the artworld' believes there *is* something significant about it, something *worth* appreciating (even though he may not be able to state exactly what this is), why should he draw attention to it in the first place? We can only assume, as in the case of Readymades, Wollheim suggests – and also, it might be added, in the case of much Post-Modern art, as I shall discuss in the next chapter – that the person in question is prompted by some other motive.

Recognition of the essentially public nature of art enables us to indicate answers to some of the questions raised at the beginning of this chapter. It will be evident, for example, that manuscripts and scores remaining unpublished, perhaps undiscovered, and choreographic inventions performed exclusively in private, are *not* art – though it is merely fortuitous that they have not so far acquired this status. Neither are songs, poems, dances, etc. as yet only 'in the composer's head' – though this time for the very different reason that they *cannot* (logically cannot) be. For whereas in the first case it is only a contingent matter that what may be art is so far not known about, yet *could* be, in the second case there is nothing in sensuous form that is available for public scrutiny. Only when these two conditions (at least) are fulfilled can something be a candidate

[2] Included in the second edition of *Art and Its Objects*.

for art status – though success is not, of course, thereby automatically guaranteed.

This is sometimes apt to strike people as rather strange. Surely, it might be said, if something is an artwork it has always been an artwork, and always will be. How can the nature of something change simply as a result of its being regarded in a particular way? But, as should now be clear, a work of art is *more* than a physical phenomenon. The same physical object (which may be a set of movements, sounds, etc.) can therefore rank as art at one period of time, but not at another; in one place, but not elsewhere. As Danto puts it:

> Not everything can be an artwork at every time: the artworld must be ready for it. Much as not every line which is *witty* in a given context can be witty in all ('Artworks and real things', p.9).

Any sense of strangeness occasioned by this idea indicates a failure to grasp the significance of what has been discussed in the last few pages, namely the social and historical character of art and the need, in any analysis of the concept, to take account of non-exhibited features of things, and of the customs and attitudes of a society in respect of certain objects and activities, the kind of *regard* in which they are held.

Once this is appreciated, however, we may begin to see how it is that such things as weapons, domestic utensils, masks, or articles of clothing, whether from the everyday life of our own or another civilisation, of our own day or of the past, may, appropriately treated, *become* art; how dances and songs, once an integral part of worship, say, or the celebration of some other occasion, can – again, appropriately treated – be, as it were, transformed, enter the domain of art. Removed from their normal context, 'artifactualised', in Dickie's rather awkward term, such phenomena can take on a different character; they can acquire a new status, a new role in the life of the society that accords them this different treatment. And that society, it may be noted, is thereby itself modified; for art not only derives its 'being' from the culture in which it emerges, but in turn contributes to, and indeed in some measure constitutes, that culture.

What, however, does 'appropriately treated' amount to here? Is it not a deplorable case of putting the cart before the horse to suggest that for certain things to be works of art it is all a matter of their being exhibited and presented in particular ways? This would seem to be the *result* of their being regarded as art rather than the means by which they are to be identified as such.[1] Do we not have to say something also about the nature of the interest and value placed on them *as* works of art? This is certainly one answer that has been proposed – and elaborated in terms of an *aesthetic* interest. But, as we shall see in the next

[1] Cf. Diffey, T. J., 'On defining art', p. 19.

chapter, this may not be a necessary (much less a sufficient) condition. Moreover something that Wollheim says about an aesthetic interest could be suggested in respect of an *artistic* interest, namely that there need not be any comprehensive way of referring to what is destinctive about it *other than* as that sort of interest (*Art and Its Objects*, pp. 91–93).

This, of course, immediately invites the charge of circularity. But it is a circularity that need not be vicious; and Wollheim reminds us in this connection of a pervasive error in our thinking to which Wittgenstein drew attention: that of identifying one phenomenon with another phenomenon more specific than it, or that of seeing everything as a diminished version of itself. Wollheim proposes then that

> the primary occurrence of the expression 'work of art' is in the phrase 'to regard x as a work of art'; (that) if we wish to understand the expression we must first understand it there.

And there is no artistic interest, he argues, that can be identified independently of the institutions of art. An artwork, that is, can be seen to be an artwork only as a result of our finding it possible to *place* it, so to speak, within the framework of an accredited body of such works. A remark of John Wisdom in a paper as yet unpublished, but quoted by Graham McFee,[1] is of interest here: 'In saying that a thing is of a certain kind, I place it. This is a form of expression we do in fact use ("I couldn't place him", "I couldn't place it")'.

As with knowledge of any kind, then, we cannot start from scratch but have to begin from where we already are, with what we already know. 'The aspiration to make *all* things new', as Renford Bambrough insists, 'is incoherent'.[2] Thus in the case of art our taking-off point has to be those instances which are meant to be seen as art, i.e. which have been produced intentionally under the concept of art (even if an individual artist may not be explicitly aware of what that concept involves or be able to articulate it). In this way we may resist that 'craving for generality' or 'the contemptuous attitude towards the particular case', as Wittgenstein puts it in *The Blue and the Brown Books* (pp. 17–18): further candidates are considered in relation to acknowledged artworks against a background of established or, we might say, inherited standards and traditions – inherited inasmuch as we are brought up in a society in which human beings engage in art activities (in the wide sense referred to earlier of creating, presenting, reviewing, collecting, etc.). But a point made during the discussion of family resemblances perhaps needs to be stressed again here, namely that to

---

[1] *Much of Jackson Pollock is Vivid Wallpaper*, p. 48. Cf. also Jones, P., 'Understanding a work of art', s.III.

[2] 'To reason is to generalise', p. 43. (Bambrough's argument is, of course, precisely *against* this assertion.)

recognise something as art is not a matter of searching for a *prescribed* set of similarities. The standards and traditions of art, far from being fixed or static, are constantly being enlarged and revised, as new dances, novels, films, operas and so on (as well as combinations of some of these) achieve the status of art, perhaps using new materials and new techniques and demanding new kinds of response and behaviour on the part of those who watch or listen or read.

Reference to what has gone on in the past as a necessary part of any satisfactory account of art does not, therefore, imply a rigid concept. Paradoxically perhaps, it is the continuity of certain cultural practices and norms that makes for its flexibility and elasticity; without them innovation would not be possible, for, as we saw earlier, traditions are necessary for there to be fresh developments. Modern dance, for example, originated as a direct consequence of classical ballet, and could be understood as a new kind of dance only against that background. Its exponents might have thought they were overthrowing everything, but they did not for some time attempt to dispense with, say, music or some other sort of sound accompaniment, or with stages, audiences who sat in their seats to watch, and the like. And while some of these conventions, along with a number of others, have from time to time been abandoned by later choreographers – especially by post-modern dancers – some connections with previous presentations remain, and have to remain (though it need not be the *same* connections that persist). Otherwise, as emphasised previously, these 'pieces' (a term preferred to 'works' by some contemporary artists) could not be seen as art at all, maybe not even as dance.

Moreover any artist is always limited not only by the nature of his medium (what can be 'said' in the dance cannot be said in literature, what is expressible in music is not expressible in sculpture, and so on); but also by the particular milieu in which that medium is used. For artistic techniques do not develop independently of the general cultural climate or of previous uses of paint, movement, words, etc.; the work of even the most highly creative artist grows out of the habits of thought and feeling integral to the society to which he belongs and the language and art forms which both shape and enshrine that thought and feeling. Thus T. S. Eliot, pointing out that William Blake uses the English language and not one of his own invention, says:

His individuality has developed in terms of the language, with the ways of experiencing, as well as of handling experience, that it involves. The mind and the sensibility he has to express are of the language ('Literature and society', pp. 186–187).

And L. R. Rogers, speaking of sculpture, puts the point in a way that applies directly to the dance:

Artists live in definite times and places and what they can conceive or invent depends very largely on the kinds of spatial organisation they are familiar with. They are inevitably limited by the habits of spatial thinking of their society and period ('Sculptural thinking', p. 202).

The fact that it is only in the light of what has already been accepted as art that new departures can be seen *as* new departures, means that newly admitted candidates – and most especially, perhaps, candidates presently seeking admission – are intelligible as art only to those with some knowledge of its history. This is not necessarily, or even usually, 'history of art' as a formal subject of study, however, but rather, firsthand acquaintance with individual artworks and art practices – in particular, of course, those belonging to the art form and the genre to which the newcomer most closely approximates. Anyone unfamiliar with Contemporary dance, for instance, would be likely to find it difficult to accommodate within the idea of art some of, say, Merce Cunningham's later pieces; but those who have followed his long career in some detail are likely to bring to their looking a store of experience that enables them to make significant comparisons such that a judgment is possible as regards their art (or non-art, or borderline art) status. Indeed the knowledgeable spectator, listener, or reader – perhaps a critic, an art historian, a collector or a biographer – can often find a certain coherence between the items of an individual artist's total output, or that of a group, better than can the artist or group concerned. It is usually the *connoisseur*[1] who is first aware of movements in art.

Conversely, it is the man- and woman-in-the-street who are apt to be most resistant to change in the arts and to be puzzled by new developments. For they have literally lost their bearings; the fewer points of reference there are to existing artworks, the more restricted and the more readily upset are people's responses and expectations. What is required in such circumstances is someone who can latch on, as it were, to what *is* familiar: to repeat, we have to start with what *can* be seen as art. But all depends, as already indicated, on both parties being able to take for granted a whole range of shared concerns and values. The would-be appreciator will be able to grasp whatever similarities and comparisons his guide may bring to his attention only in so far as he is at home in the cultural milieu within which such similarities and comparisons make sense.

However, if highly-specialised guides are constantly required by those who are already well acquainted with a particular art form, i.e. those who make up the factions and coteries with which, as Wollheim observes, art is surrounded (usually, he adds, for worse, though sometimes for better)[2], this may indicate

[1] Cf. M. Dufrenne's use of 'savant' in his Commentary on R. K. Elliott's 'The critic and the lover of art'.

[2] *Art and Its Objects*, p. 166.

that art is indeed in a sorry plight. That this is precisely the situation today, and that (as prophesied by Hegel), art is bringing about its own death, is strenuously argued by Ruby Meager in a paper, 'Art and beauty' (in which she sets out to show that art can operate as a form of life in a sense different from that discussed by Wollheim – though still ascribable, she claims, to Wittgenstein). For the individual artist, saddled with what she calls 'the awful onus of spontaneity and originality', is obliged in order to survive to attract to himself critics who alone have the time 'so to immerse themselves in his work that like sensitive midwives they can deliver this strange offspring . . . to the patient public. . . .' (p. 103).

Once the point is established that the central cases of art are those intentionally produced under the concept of art, another of the questions posed at the beginning of this chapter may be taken up, namely the possibility of art among animals (other than humans). For it now becomes evident that such a suggestion is hardly plausible. Certainly an observer or listener may find marks or movements or sounds made by birds, insects, etc. *aesthetically* interesting ('made' even in the loose sense of 'brought about unintentionally', as, for example, tracks in the snow). Indeed such marks and so on might be displayed by humans, sometimes in conditions normally reserved for art. But we cannot attribute *artistic* activity to non-human animals even in the case of, say, the singing of birds[1] or whales, or the movements and paint daubings of apes when these are intentionally produced and seem to be selected and arranged in some manner. For we are unable to say whether the intention and ordering in question involve the idea of making and presenting something which is primarily to be looked at or listened to, something which is typically altered, revised, improved upon or even scrapped altogether in order to make a better song, dance, painting or whatever.

The possibility of *dis*satisfaction on the part of an artist in respect of the look or sound of what he is doing is in fact as important as is that of satisfaction. In other words, critical appreciation goes hand in hand with making and performing: the artist pays attention to what he does not only (normally) in terms of taking care with his movements, marks or sounds, but also in terms of *what* emerges – how, say, one phrase fits with another, how repetition, contrasts, pauses, etc. make for certain effects. He himself looks or listens reflectively, discriminatingly, and proceeds in the light of this assessment; he knows what he is doing and is able to imagine how others might respond. That is, he works against the background of certain criteria – though not, as I shall discuss in a

---

[1] For an illuminating discussion of birdsong in this connection, see Scruton, R., *The Aesthetics of Architecture*, p. 80ff.

later chapter, a set of fixed criteria that can be laid down in advance, but criteria applied in relation to *this* particular effort.

Both his making and his looking or listening then take place not *in vacuo*, but in the light of other experiences – other sounds, marks and movements that he himself has seen and heard, and that he has noticed other people – especially those known as *artists* – looking at and listening to, as well as talking about, displaying and presenting in particular ways: in short, against the background of what he has learned to conceive of as art. As a social activity of this kind, art is clearly outside the range of non-language users. Conversely, *we* cannot know fully or precisely what significance the rhythmic and patterned sounds of birds or dolphins, or the hopping, stamping and whirling of apes, for example, has for them. Langer, rightly critical of Sachs here on the origins of art (she points out that he grossly over-simplifies the problem and mis-reads the 'evidence' he adduces for his proposed solution), writes:

> We do not know that the apes experience only lively fun as they trot around a post; perhaps some fickle forerunner of mystical excitement awakens in them at the moment. Perhaps their antics are merely playful. . . . We know too little to infer anything from 'the dance of the apes' (*Feeling and Form*, p. 191n.)

This last remark, however, must not be misinterpreted. It would be quite wrong to suppose that if only we found out more about apes (say), we should be in a position to know whether or not they engage in art; for this is not an empirical, but a conceptual matter, involving, as I have tried to show, criteria that rule out non-humans. Langer rightly refers, in her discussion of the differences between animal rituals (among other things) and genuine art forms, to 'the momentousness of the step from one to the other' (p. 179). Similarly, it would be mistaken to imagine that if, as she speculates, Köhler's apes carried out their performance as a result of watching human dancers, what they were imitating (however exactly in terms of steps, gestures, etc.) was a *dance*; for to do this requires more than copying a set of physical movements. An ape is no more *dancing* in the sense in which a human being dances than is a budgerigar *talking* when it imitates sounds of human speech. For that matter, neither is a human being dancing if he merely reproduces movements taken out of any context that makes those movements intelligible as dance.

To have a grasp of the concept of art, however, is not (as also with many other concepts) an all-or-nothing affair: there can be degrees of understanding, ranging from the rudimentary to the more fully-fledged; and it seems clear that this is a concept that goes on developing throughout childhood and, indeed, beyond. Even those individuals who go on to learn very little about art inevitably absorb a good deal about the forms and traditions of their own culture or sub-culture – especially in an age when television brings not only dances, plays, films, etc. into almost every home, but also news, informative talks and so forth, about such phenomena.

Thus, as Diffey suggests in 'The idea of art', while few people might be said to *possess* this idea – are able, that is, to give an account of art – many are nevertheless *possessed by* it: it is a *regulative* idea, one that permeates our experience and plays an important part in shaping it. Indeed if art were to die out in a particular society, that society would not remain the same except for that single change: the whole fabric of its customs and practices, its habits of feeling and thinking, would be radically altered. Wollheim is therefore right to insist, when commenting on Hegel's speculation that art might disappear from the world, that in such an event 'many aspects of social existence would have to be unravelled to an extent that exceeds our imaginative powers' (*Art and Its Objects*, p. 104).

The way then in which debate about art tends to flow freely back and forth among specialists and non-specialists alike, with examples and counter-examples readily produced to defeat proffered generalisations and definitions, indicates that the answer to the question 'What is art?' is, in some sense, already known. Wollheim once more:

> We all do have such experience of poetry, painting, music, etc. that, if we cannot (as I am sure we cannot) say on the basis of it what these things are, we can at least recognize when we are being told that they are something which in point of fact they are not (p. 3).

That is, the question presupposes that examples of art have already been identified. Moreover, as will have been evident throughout this chapter, we are also able to take for granted a great deal about art in general – for instance, that it is a complex phenomenon; that its manifestations are amazingly diverse; that it constantly undergoes change and has (as we saw Weitz could not avoid assuming), an expansive, adventurous character; and so on.

It has also become clear that the status of artworks is determined not by philosophical definition, but by history: as Diffey puts it, 'anybody who thinks that he can freely define art as takes his fancy has taken leave of reality – historical reality' ('On defining art', p. 19). Nevertheless, as he further argues in 'The Republic of Art', there are occasions, especially in periods (such as our own) when the arts are subject to rapid change, when the question whether something is a work of art is not an idle one. For while this has *normally* been settled, it does not follow that the decision can *never* be contested, though neither does the successful contesting of a particular case mean that *nothing* is settled (p. 147). There is thus every reason why philosophers should continue to pursue their enquiries into the question 'What is art?' – just as there is every reason why, although we all (in some sense) know a person when we meet one, the highly important question 'What is a person?' remains worth pursuing (cf. 'Essentialism and the definition of "art" ', pp. 114–115).

The concept of art then would certainly seem to be a classic case of the sort Gallie[1] has proposed is 'essentially complex and essentially contested' – a concept, that is, lacking full elaboration, yet nevertheless in general use. It is one that does not *as it happens* occasion endless disputes (for example, on account of psychological differences between people), but is *in the nature of the case* contestable; and will, as a rule, actually be contested. Moreover this contestedness, Gallie maintains, is recognised by the various disputants, who deliberately use the term in question in a particular way in direct opposition to other uses. Nevertheless what he calls 'the persistent vagueness' of 'art', 'history', 'democracy', .etc., far from counting adversely against such concepts, is positively in their favour. For although not resolvable by argument, they are sustained by argument; they are essentially *appraisive* concepts, involving some kind of valued achievement which always admits of variation and modification. They therefore benefit, rather than suffer, from the constant scrutiny to which they are subjected; we are regularly obliged to consider what they mean, to debate this use or that. Indeed if, as Gallie suggests, we should hear about a society whose responses to art showed a high degree of uniformity,

> we should be inclined to say that, however *artistically gifted* some of its members might be, its artistic life . . . was of an unhappily stinted kind ('Art as an essentially contested concept', p. 114).

The question might even arise, he adds, whether in our sense of the term they had an adequate appreciation of works of art at all.

We might wonder, however, whether they *had* such works, or at any rate a concept of art that would enable *us* to identify as artworks the things and performances in question.

Suggestions for further reading on institutional theories of art
Aagaard-Mogensen, L. (ed.), *Culture and Art*.
Blizek, W. L., 'An institutional theory of art'.
Cohen, T., 'The possibility of art: remarks on a proposal by Dickie'.
Dickie, G., *Art and the Aesthetic: An Institutional Analysis*.
McGregor, R., 'Dickie's institutionalised aesthetic'.
Sclafani, R., 'Artworks, art theory, and the artworld'.

[1] 'Essentially contested concepts' (published, like 'Art as an essentially contested concept', in 1956).

CHAPTER FIVE

Art and aesthetic experience

> When one is talking about the arts seriously, the focus upon the aesthetic aspect of art . . . is *logically* necessary if the talk is really to be about *art*.
>
> L. Arnaud Reid: *Meaning in the Arts*

> Aesthetic qualities are neither a necessary nor a sufficient condition of arthood.
>
> T. Binkley: 'Deciding about art'

In philosophical discussions to do with the classification of knowledge and experience, a mode of awareness that is often claimed to be of a unique kind is that relating to art and the aesthetic.[1] There are, however, two notions here; but the question of their boundaries and of the nature of the relation between them receives in the main far less consideration than, in my view, it deserves.[2] Indeed it seems all too often taken for granted that there is not only (as we saw in Chapter 2) a historical, but also a logical, connection between art and the aesthetic.

In this chapter, therefore, I shall take a preliminary look at this issue before going on to examine the concept of the aesthetic in greater detail, with particular reference to the dance. It might, of course, be suggested that such an examination should be conducted first. Nevertheless, because of the long association in philosophical aesthetics between the aesthetic and art, the propriety of which has been challenged only during the second half of this century, it may be useful to start by considering the two concepts together, each as we seem initially to think of them perhaps throwing some light on the other.

It might be noted to begin with that the term 'aesthetic', in contrast to 'art', has only a limited currency in everyday speech, although Jerome Stolnitz was surely going too far in his paper 'On the origins of "aesthetic disinterested-ness"', when he claimed (albeit in 1961) that the British never use the word 'aesthetic' or 'aesthetics'. But he was quite right to remind us that it was not the British who invented these terms. As we have already seen, 'aesthetic' is a philosophical coinage originating in the eighteenth century, and it still remains a largely technical or semi-technical concept having its natural home in philosophy and heavily laden with historical overtones.

---

[1] See, for example, Reid, L. A., *Ways of Knowledge and Experience*; Oakeshott, M., 'The voice of poetry in the conversation of mankind'; Hirst, P. H., 'Liberal education and the nature of knowledge'.

[2] See, however, Best, D., 'The aesthetic and the artistic' (published after this chapter was written).

Similarly with the term 'aesthetic judgment', though whereas such a judgment was traditionally construed very narrowly, typically of the form 'x is beautiful', it today extends in its application to a great variety of qualities. Moreover while it is apt to sound as if someone is sitting in judgment, passing judgment on something, or, as Wollheim[1] puts it (in respect of art), taking a schoolmaster's view of whatever is in question, 'aesthetic judgment' is used not so much in connection with grading or rating an object or performance, i.e. comparing its *merits* with other objects or performances, as with appraising, assessing, evaluating, or appreciating it in the sense of discerning its character as a particular (cf. Diffey's remarks in 'Evaluation and aesthetic appraisals', p. 367). It might further be observed that in philosophy generally the term 'judgment' is rather less widely used than it was formerly, some philosophers in fact regarding it as having a decidedly old-fashioned ring. In the main, therefore, I shall speak of aesthetic *appraisal* and *appraisals*.

Outside philosophy 'aesthetic' continues, it would seem, to retain something of its original associations with, first, the idea of the beautiful, and secondly, that of pleasure – especially (though mistakenly, I shall maintain), pleasure of a sensuous kind, such as that involved in stroking fur or plunging into the sea on a hot day. The term 'aesthetic' is, of course, used quite extensively in relation to the arts – sometimes, indeed, it is used carelessly, even by philosophers, as the equivalent of 'artistic'. But it also occurs fairly regularly in connection with appreciation of nature, of sport, dress, interior design, and so on; and sometimes, though perhaps less often nowadays, it carries the suggestion of a special attitude towards life as a whole consisting in a devotion to beauty and the arts as overriding values, often in opposition to other values and hence divorced from them.

Such an attitude was at the centre of the 'art for art's sake' movement, or *aestheticism*, which flourished during the mid-to-late nineteenth century, particularly in the fields of literature and painting. More accurately termed 'art for aesthetics' sake', as Diffey points out in the paper just mentioned, this movement involved taking a radical stand against assumptions about, and demands for, moral teaching in art. What mattered, its adherents protested, was that artworks should be beautiful; any other interest or function they might have was seen as entirely superfluous, even detrimental to their value as art. Indeed, in its most extreme form, the doctrine laid down that art not only need not, but must not, serve any extra-aesthetic ends whatsoever.

This association of the aesthetic with aestheticism and aesthetes, a specimen of whom was frequently depicted as 'an affected young gentleman with long hair, velveteen jacket and knickerbockers, attended by admiring, languidly

---

[1] Philosophy and the arts', p. 225.

ethereal young ladies',[1] has no doubt been responsible for a good deal of the misunderstanding, suspicion and even hostility that has often attached to the aesthetic, and that to some extent has carried over to art. It partly accounts, for example, for the still quite widespread conception of classical ballet as a somewhat effeminate activity for men and boys.

Yet whether or not the concept of the aesthetic is vague, esoteric or merely dormant in the popular consciousness, and whatever the various uses or misuses the term may have, it might nevertheless be suggested that ordinary language does support the attempt to locate a special category of experience – perhaps of understanding – that philosophers, at any rate, refer to as *aesthetic*. For we have a group of words, among which are *lovely, pretty, graceful, elegant, hideous, ungainly, grotesque* and, most notably, *beautiful* and *ugly*, that seem to have a particular function as they are commonly applied, on the one hand, to natural phenomena such as rainbows, butterflies, flowers, landscapes, the forms and movement of animals (including those of humans), and, on the other, dances, paintings, pieces of music, vases and other artifacts such as cathedrals, furniture, cars, bridges, ships, and so forth.

A further consideration that might seem to lend support to a general intuition that there is a distinctively aesthetic mode of awareness or way of appraising things, has to do with the idea of enjoying something *for its own sake*, as we (somewhat puzzlingly) say – an idea that is crucial, as I see it, to an understanding of the concept of the aesthetic. Thus whereas, for example, we might take an interest in a plot of land for, say, building purposes, or as a source of food, or as a place where athletes might train, it is possible instead simply to admire it for the view, to enjoy this in its own right, for no other reason.

Again, while many dances, songs, pieces of sculpture and such like might be appreciated for the expertise and craftsmanship they display, for their psychological or moral insights, or for their political or religious or social relevance, there is a tendency to feel that they are not to be appreciated only, sometimes not at all, in terms of these other categories of understanding, that they are of value in some way that in not reducible to any other. It has, indeed, been reigning orthodoxy in aesthetic philosophy until comparatively recently that while many artworks may, and often do, have a variety of uses and beneficial effects, and may represent superb achievements of skill, such uses or effects or features are not what constitute their unique character. To make the point negatively: if someone regards dancing, for instance, *simply* as a source of erotic pleasure, an exhibition of highly skilled movement, a means of keeping fit or providing emotional relief, or as affording the opportunity for making social contacts, he is not, it has been insisted, approaching it as *art*.

The use (or as some might say, misuse, even abuse) of music as a trigger for

[1] Johnson, R. V., *Aestheticism*, p. 9. This is a very useful text on the subject.

personal reverie – for reasons external to the work itself – is vividly captured by Dannie Abse in his poem *Sunday Evening*, which begins:

> Loved not for themselves those tenors who sing
> arias from 'Aïda' on horned, tinny
> gramophones – but because they take a man back
> to a half forgotten thing,

and which goes on to express the self-indulgence of listening to music in order to 'recall some other place, another time/now charmingly outmoded':

> What, for wrong motives, too often is approved
> proves we once existed, becomes mere flattery
> – then it's ourselves whom we are listening to,
> and, by hearing, we are moved.
>
> (Collected Poems, 1958–76)

To listen to (or to play) music, as also to dance or look at a dance, a film, a painting, etc., purely for purposes of reminiscence or for its theoretical or utilitarian interest is not, then, it has been argued (or perhaps merely assumed), to focus on the work *as* an artwork; though this has not been to say that it is impossible to respond to something from a variety of points of view on one and the same occasion (well brought out in J. O. Urmson's paper, 'What makes a situation aesthetic?' sections 7, 8 and 9). One's interest in a dance or a house, for instance, might simultaneously be historical, economic, *and* aesthetic – 'multiply-grounded', in Urmson's phrase. Nevertheless if appreciation can be exclusively aesthetic, this means that there must be some way in which it is distinguishable from any other.

The idea, however, that it is possible, let alone usual, to value a work of art in its own right, without concern for any further interest it has, or might have, would have been largely incomprehensible before the eighteenth century. Indeed the concept of art as it is widely understood in the Western world today was unknown to Classical Antiquity, the Middle Ages, and the Renaissance alike. The Latin term *ars*, for example (Greek equivalent, *techne*), was applied to a great variety of activities and pursuits which included not only some of those we now class as fine art (such as sculpture), but also both what we usually regard as crafts (such as the work of glass-blowers or stone-masons) and disciplines such as the physical sciences, logic, and certain branches of mathematics.[1] All these activities were seen as involving knowledge of a kind capable of precise formulation by reference to rules or principles: art was that

---

[1] See Tatarkiewicz, W., 'Classification of arts in antiquity'; and Kristeller, P. O., 'The modern system of the arts', s.II.

which could be well done according to a blueprint or formula. By contrast poetry, music, and the dance were excluded, since these were thought of as involving no such knowledge, but as dependent on inspiration. Art is thus a concept that has undergone changes of both expansion and contraction; and from approximately the fifth century B.C. to the sixteenth A. D. artifacts and activities that we now think of as art were valued chiefly for their religious or didactic or social functions, or for the excellence of their workmanship.

With the development in the eighteenth century of the idea of art as a discrete mode of interest, involving the enjoying of artworks aesthetically, went changes therefore in the way in which various objects and activities were grouped together under the heading of 'art'. It was not so much that techniques and ideas within art forms themselves altered (though that happened too), as that the arts came to be regarded as occupying a different place in relation to other activities and modes of experience, and as playing a different role than formerly in the life of society as a whole. For instance a radical change of outlook was required in order for sculpture to become dissociated from, say, carpentry, and to be associated instead with poetry, music and the dance.[1] Such a change took place only gradually; but it was a change that was already gaining some momentum during the late seventeenth as well as the early eighteenth century, especially in France (where, it may be noted, the dance had already become established as a theatre spectacle rather earlier, with an Academy of the Dance set up in 1661 – a few years, interestingly enough, before an Academy of Music). Thus Baumgarten and other German as well as British philosophers whose writings on the aesthetic and art came after his *Aesthetica* could take for granted the classification of the arts worked out by Batteux in 1746; and that system, founded as it was on the idea that what was common to the fine arts was beauty, might be seen as pointing forward to the notion of art as something to be valued for itself.

Before the relationship between art and the aesthetic is further explored, however, it is necessary to say something more about the latter. We might return at this point, therefore, to the two considerations which it was tentatively suggested earlier might seem to indicate a mode of awareness – the aesthetic – that is qualitatively different from any other: on the one hand, the idea of enjoying things for their own sake and, on the other, a vocabulary of what seem to be specifically aesthetic terms. For it might be thought possible to identify and describe this mode either by focusing on the nature of the response of the experiencing subject, or by trying to find some principle by which a set of qualities or features of objects, commonly labelled 'beautiful', 'ugly', etc. may be understood as *aesthetic* qualities. The history of aesthetic enquiry does in fact reveal just such a readiness to concentrate on one or other of these two

[1] Cf. Tatarkiewicz, W., 'What is art? The problem of definition today'.

approaches, the first often characterised as 'subjective', the second as 'objective' (assuming that the subjective/objective contrast is here intuitively clear). But, as I shall try to show in more detail in ensuing chapters, neither approach proves satisfactory on its own.

At least two sets of problems present themselves in connection with the first – that is, an account in terms of the mental state of the aesthetically involved person (for example, the postulating of some specifically aesthetic emotion). To begin with, there is the difficulty of correctly identifying such a state of mind, of distinguishing it from other states. For it is impossible to discover the nature of aesthetic awareness (or, for that matter, any other kind) by endeavouring to look inside ourselves, as it were.[1] There is just no means of getting at 'inner' experience, or of ensuring that we have not made a mistake, in the absence of its expression in observable behaviour, and unless at the same time it is possible to identify and describe some objectively verifiable feature of the environment with which it is connected.

Moreover if aesthetic awareness constitutes a mode of understanding, this connection cannot be merely contingent; otherwise such awareness could be simply a sensation *caused* by an object (the word 'object' here, and throughout in this context, understood as including an event, activity, performance, etc.). Far from being a passive reaction produced by some merely accidental circumstance, aesthetic interest, it will be argued, involves a certain conception of something on the part of an actively experiencing person; and we cannot discover or characterise his mental state in isolation from the object towards which his attention is directed – or, more precisely, the object as he conceives it: to use a philosophical term, the *intentional object* (from the Latin, *intendere*, to aim; cf. our use of 'object' in 'the object of his admiration, envy', etc.).

Further, to speak of a mode of understanding is to speak of what is available to others besides oneself, and thus subject to public standards. So if aesthetic appraisal is of a distinctive kind, a satisfactory account cannot be subjective in the sense that implies a wholly private, idiosyncratic response, incapable of support (or refutation) by reasons. In such an event, rational discussion would be rendered impossible and aesthetic discriminations reduced to the level of preferences for, say, one sort of food or drink rather than another, this sort of bodily sensation rather than that. Such preferences, however, seem importantly different: it would be odd to suggest, for instance, that someone who likes cider but not beer, or the sensations of surf-riding but not of ski-ing, lacks *understanding* in one case but not in the other; or, further, that he could be reasoned into or out of his predilections. But if he finds, say, Twyla Tharp's *Eight Jelly Rolls* witty, or York Minster fine, we are in a realm of values which, in contrast to desires or sensations, are amenable to reasons; like his beliefs, emotions and

---

[1] This is well discussed by Best in *Expression in Movement and the Arts*.

actions, an individual's aesthetic responses may (I shall maintain), be changed by a process of reasoning.

The other approach too runs into difficulties. In the first place, the group of seemingly special aesthetic terms we have is both too wide and too narrow. 'Beautiful', for example, may be used with reference to a great variety of qualities, ranging from sensuous charm (as with much of the poetry of Spenser and Keats, or Richard Alston's *Tiger Balm*, for instance), to the lyrical and flowing (e.g. Alvin Ailey's *Lark Ascending* and the Vaughan Williams' music that accompanies it); from the neat and economical (e.g. the rhyming couplets of many Shakespeare sonnets) to that which (like much Greek sculpture or José Limón's *A Choreographic Offering*), is harmonious in the sense of classically proportioned (summed up in the sixteenth-century Latin tag, *pulchrum est quid commensuratum est*: 'that is beautiful which is in proportion'). By contrast, 'beautiful' may indicate something seen as peculiarly well fitted for its purpose, or as a perfect specimen of its kind – hence Thomas De Quincey's talk of a beautiful ulcer in his entertaining essay, 'On murder considered as one of the fine arts'.

On the other hand the collection of terms in question is altogether inadequate for a number of things that often occasion what seems to be an aesthetic response – the stark, melancholy quality of a bare hillside, for example, or the desolate, haunting cry of the great northern diver; the flamboyant or meticulous gestures of an orchestral conductor, or the stormy 'music' of wind and waves. And if we turn to art, there is a host of works both of our own time and of the past that might more appropriately be described as unified, ironic, anguished, serene, and such like, than in terms of beauty or ugliness and their cognates.

Any attempt to locate a set of distinctively aesthetic qualities – quite apart from the elementary error that might underlie it, namely of supposing that for every word there exists some corresponding entity – encounters a yet more serious problem. This concerns the logical status of qualities such as beauty, grace, hideousness (not to mention unity, irony, and so on); for these features are not, it is usually assumed, observable in the way that are, say, greenness, loudness or angularity. The nature of this distinction, which will occupy us at some length in later chapters, is of long-standing philosophical interest, of course. For Baumgarten, it will be recalled, beauty was a property of things when perceived as wholes, while certain other philosophers of the period who belonged to the British empirical tradition regarded beauty and ugliness as features requiring for their perception the exercise of a special mental faculty, the faculty of *taste* (known by some as an 'inner sense'), which was supposed to function in a way analogous to that of the 'external' senses.

But now, we may note, the experiencing subject has been brought more prominently into the account; and even greater importance was accorded to the individual in actively structuring his experience by later philosophers who followed Kant's revolutionary work in epistemology towards the end of the eighteenth century. Thus, instead of being thought of as existing independently of a perceiving subject, beauty (and other aesthetic qualities) came to be regarded by many philosophers as intimately connected with the person's mental stance – his attitude or disposition towards the object in question. That is, rather than aesthetic appreciation being understood as a matter of *recognising* something as, say, graceful or pretty, as it might be recognised as symmetric or tiny or curved, the idea gained ground that such appreciation involves an active, personal response to whatever is being attended to, and that a convincing analysis of this mode of awareness must accommodate both a subjective *and* an objective element.

There are, however, differing versions of 'aesthetic attitude' theories; and to what extent the individual is responsible for the nature of his experience has been, and continues to remain, a controversial issue.[1] In some accounts the adopting of a special stance is a necessary condition of access to certain objective features of things – aesthetic features. In others, it is the means whereby an aesthetic character is imposed on objects; it is not so much that qualities such as beauty are revealed, as in some way constituted, by this attitude – by, for example, an act of imaginative attention. On the first view an objective reality becomes available to the percipient under certain (logical) conditions: hence not everything can have aesthetic qualities. On the second type of theory the individual is placed in complete control so that anything, at least in principle, can become an object of aesthetic regard. The range of aesthetic experience is thus enlarged and, correspondingly, rather less prominence is given to beauty.

Nevertheless attitude accounts in general usually contain reference to the arresting and focusing of attention on something in the external world, i.e. to direct, firsthand experience; pleasure or satisfaction in that thing for its own sake – an affective response involving the apprehension of its form; and an absence of either theoretical or practical interest in the object – in other words, a lack of concern with its causes or consequences, or with its possible ends or purposes. Unhampered, at least temporarily, by the duties and commitments of day-to-day living, which in the main is dominated by thinking in terms of means and ends, making plans, taking decisions, and so forth, the aesthetically interested person (so most accounts go) is in some way lifted above his everyday situation: his experience is, in the popular phrase, 'out of this world'. In the language of some aesthetic attitude theories, he is engaged in an act of disinterested contemplation: movement, colour, sound, etc. are of intrinsic interest; fictitious characters, events and situations are enjoyed in their own right, for themselves.

---

[1] See, for example, Dickie, G., *Art and the Aesthetic*, ch. 2.

In recent decades, however, the notion of disinterested contemplation has incurred considerable scepticism and hostility among a number of philosophers (as well as some artists). Indeed the whole idea of an aesthetic attitude has progressively come under attack from a variety of quarters. Dickie, for instance, has written a paper, 'The myth of the aesthetic attitude'; for others it is a possibility but rare, Charlton arguing in 'Aestheticism' that it is a somewhat unreal abstraction that trivialises aesthetic experience; while Beardsley, hastening to its defence in 'Aesthetic experience regained', has expressed the fear that the aesthetic point of view is 'a concept that has lost its respectability in sophisticated circles, and is in peril of its very life' (p.4).

Certainly a variety of difficulties occurs in connection with the ideas mentioned above, sometimes partly on account of the manner in which they are expressed. There is often, for example, talk of *appearances*, the *perceptual object*, the *art image*, or, in Langer's ghostly-sounding terminology, the *apparition* or *semblance*; and sometimes the appearance of the object in question is spoken of in such a way as to suggest that that object is actually something else, that behind the appearance there is some ineffable reality, while our ordinary space-time world is an illusion. Thus considerable puzzlement arises as to how aesthetic perception might be thought to relate to normal perception; and this puzzlement is apt to be deepened by a preoccupation on the part of many aestheticians with the visual (there is in fact a long tradition among theorists of *beauty* to concentrate almost exclusively on objects of sight – indeed St. Thomas Aquinas defined beauty as 'that which pleases the eye').

Imagination too is a highly complex concept, and one might wonder how a distinction is to be drawn between imaginative activity in the aesthetic situation and in, say, science or history or philosophy. Equally problematic is the notion of *pleasure* (or *enjoyment, satisfaction, delight*, etc.); for it might be supposed that in aesthetic experience nothing more is involved than either enjoying *oneself* during, say, dancing or watching a performance (cf. Abse's poem referred to earlier); or pleasure of an intellectual kind such as that derived from an elegant piece of deduction in mathematics or philosophical argument; or (as already mentioned) sensuous delight in the gratification of some antecedent desire or appetite; and so on. On the other hand care is needed to avoid circularity – to avoid saying, in effect, that aesthetic enjoyment involves an interest in aesthetic qualities; aesthetic qualities are those that give rise to aesthetic enjoyment. Moreover even to speak of *aesthetic* pleasure may be misleading, for it is apt to suggest that there is a particular kind of pleasure that somehow *feels* different from any other sort.

Again, whenever *form* is spoken of in connection with art or aesthetic appreciation the danger of ambiguity, vagueness, and obscurity looms large. Noting another troublesome concept, John Martin remarks in his *Introduction to the Dance*:

As soon as rhythm is mentioned, we are likely to find ourselves enveloped in as dense a fog of mysticism and vagueness as that which beclouds the subject of form itself (p. 67).

Perhaps most in need of elucidation are the notions of *disinterested contemplation* and *for its own sake*. For if the suggestion is that aesthetic interest is self-contained, having no aim or end external to itself, no connection or significance with matters outside or beyond, it might well be doubted whether, and in what way, it is any different from play – play of a rather superior or refined sort, perhaps, yet nevertheless only a kind of 'game', unrelated to the serious business of living.

Many of these questions touch on indisputably difficult issues (taken up in more detail in later chapters). But it is not only the intelligibility of the concept of the aesthetic that gives rise to concern; it is also its relevance, if any, for art. Most philosophers who have expressed dissatisfaction and scepticism with regard to the idea of aesthetic appreciation have, in fact, been motivated primarily by a concern for art and art criticism; for our response to many artworks, they insist, is not exclusively, or even mainly, an aesthetic response. To identify artistic qualities with aesthetic qualities is therefore to place unjustifiable limits on the meaning(s) of a work; and to ignore its *non*-aesthetic aspects is often to ignore that work's chief values. This is perhaps especially true of philosophers with a particular interest in literature and drama, where moral, political or psychological considerations, for example, are frequently among the most important.

In 'Aesthetic and personal qualities', for instance, Colin Lyas argues that a tendency to slip from that use of 'aesthetic' which concerns *any* interest in the arts to that use which concerns a certain range of qualities such as grace, balance, or proportion – qualities that can be ascribed both to artworks and to natural phenomena – can have dangerous consequences for purposes of understanding and evaluating art. For if artworks are put on the same footing as natural phenomena, qualities such as profundity, humour, glibness, that do not and could not belong to natural objects (nor typically, it might be added, to sporting activities) may be overlooked. Indeed in another paper, 'Personal qualities and the intentional fallacy', Lyas goes so far as to claim that if we are to explain the importance of art we must suppose it to have values *additional* to any aesthetic values it can share with natural phenomena.

Everything depends here, of course, on what are to count as *aesthetic* qualities (investigated more thoroughly in the next chapter). Lyas (for one) adopts a rather narrow, though not always consistent view, identifying them sometimes with 'surface' or 'sensuous surface' qualities (e.g. smoothness of texture and sound, vividness of colour), sometimes with formal qualities and that small group that includes elegance, grace, and the like. A similarly restricted conception is also not uncommon, in my experience, among many people interested in the dance. There has certainly been considerable hostility towards the aesthetic among a number of modern dancers, although this is perhaps hardly surprising given the background of the concept, as sketched above, and some of the ideas with which (even if mistakenly) it has come to be associated.

It has indeed seemed to some twentieth-century artists that aesthetic qualities are not merely of limited interest for art, but undesirable. The notion of the beautiful in particular was repugnant, though understandably so, to those dancers whose concern it was, in Martin's famous, though somewhat misleading phrase, 'to externalise personal, authentic experience',[1] and to reveal the agonies and grimness of life as well as its joys and comedies. For the pioneers of the 'new' twentieth-century dance both of Central Europe and of the United States *aesthetic* was exemplified by the classical ballet of the late nineteenth century, with its sentimental prettiness, its formal decorativeness, and its often rather mechanical exhibition of sheer virtuosity and bodily skill.

Writing of Kurt Jooss' work in particular, Coton, for example, insisted that modern theatre dance was 'not confined to what we call gracefulness of the body and general beauty of line and rhythm in the movements' (*The New Ballet*, p. 29). It is not entirely clear what he means when he goes on to say that 'the intention is to give an image of the various forces of life in their everlasting interplay; that is, a manifestation of Nature' (dancers and dance theorists of the period were much given to talk of 'forces of life' and of 'Nature' – with a capital N!). But in so far as Coton is probably thinking of the wide range of movement of which the human body is capable and, with that, of expression, his mention of an *image* suggests that in fact there need not be any conflict at all here between what he is claiming for the 'new' dance and what I shall maintain is importantly involved in aesthetic appreciation. His contrast here is merely between beauty and other qualities of movement.

Alternatively, or sometimes as well, the overtones of the 'art for art's sake' doctrine were (and are) understandably anathema to those for whom the dance, and indeed all art, should be concerned with offering a comment on life and the human condition, especially with conveying some sort of social, political, moral, or religious message. Many of Jooss' ballets in the 1930s, for instance, were unashamedly didactic – though as artistically powerful in that respect as on any other grounds. Coton was quite explicit in this connection:

Man's chief interest is, still, Man; and this interest can be stimulated and rewarded by the arts in proportion to their ability to shed light on his

---

[1] *The Modern Dance*, p. 19 (*misleading* in that 'externalise' suggests that some fully-fledged 'inner' feeling or thought exists *prior* to its expression).

problems, teach him philosophic lessons and direct his moral leanings (p. 25).

But again, neither Jooss' nor his contemporaries' concern with social and political issues in the dance, nor that of later choreographers in the United States and elsewhere, is necessarily incompatible with a view of art that involves the aesthetic. For the idea that for something to *be* art it must be regarded aesthetically does not entail that aesthetic considerations *alone* are relevant to artistic appreciation. The question of whether, *in a particular case*, a work is less interesting for its aesthetic than, say, its moral or psychological aspects (a question for the critic) has, then, to be distinguished from the *general* question (a question for philosophy) of whether an aesthetic interest is necessary at all.

Nevertheless underlying any judgment about the relative importance of a work's aesthetic qualities is the assumption that such qualities are of *some* value, even if only minimal: a conceptual connection between art and the aesthetic is therefore not ruled out. But if someone were to claim that, say, a certain dance was of *no* aesthetic interest whatever, yet that he regarded it as art, he would be denying (either explicitly or implicitly) any such connection.

This would be to take a much more radical stance. It would be in effect to challenge a long-accepted tenet of aesthetic philosophy, namely that the concept of the aesthetic is central to the concept of art. P. F. Strawson, in an influential paper of the mid-1960s, 'Aesthetic appraisal and works of art', states the orthodox view as follows:

> . . . the concepts 'work of art' and 'aesthetic assessment' are logically coupled and move together, in the sense that it would be self-contradictory to speak of judging something *as a work of art* but not from the aesthetic point of view (p. 183).[1]

Thus he finds it would be odd to say, 'He didn't really judge it as a painting; he judged it from a narrowly aesthetic point of view', whereas it would not be at all odd to say, 'He was judging it from a purely aesthetic point of view; he was not judging it as a game of football'.

This assumption that the relation of art to the aesthetic is of a logical kind has, however, been questioned in recent years – partly, perhaps, owing to developments in various art forms, in particular what has broadly come to be known as Post-Modern art: forms such as Minimal art and its offshoot, Conceptual art, Events, Body art, Ludic art, etc. (Although there are a number of differences between these various manifestations, they are not significant for the

---

[1] Page numbers refer to this paper as reprinted in Strawson's collection of essays, *Freedom and Resentment*.

purposes of this discussion, and I am bracketing them together here; similar points apply to Happenings, Environmental art, and so forth.) Indeed these new forms which sprang into violent life in the United States, Germany, France, Italy and elsewhere in the 1960s and 1970s – though their ideological ancestors may be traced back to much earlier in the century – were inspired by a doctrinaire fervour to challenge and radically alter ideas about art as it had generally been understood in the West for the previous two hundred years or more.

It was not so much that the artists concerned set out to revolutionise techniques of, say, painting or dancing, or methods of composition and presentation, in the way that earlier pioneers had striven for innovation. Rather they sought to shake the very foundations of belief and practice on which art had for so long been assumed to rest – to question, and to try to force others to question, the nature of art; the notion of an art*work*; the character and function of the artist's activity; what it is to *make* a work (in philosophical terms, what is the meaning of 'work' within the phrase 'work of art'[1]); the habitual responses and expectations of audiences; the practices of critics; and a good deal more connected with the world of fine art. In particular it was their mission to break down what they saw as barriers between art and reality, art and life.

There has thus been a wholesale rejection in some quarters of the idea that an artist creates a work of imagination existing not in actual, but (to use a term of Langer) in *virtual* space and/or time, and that this work requires in turn an imaginative response from those engaged in its contemplation; that it constitutes a world of its own, different from the familiar, everyday world; that powerful feelings of wonder, delight and the like are aroused in those who watch or listen or read; and so on.

To suggest then that what such individuals are trying to achieve when, in the name of art, they simply lie down on the floor, walk about, or perform mundane tasks as in ordinary life, display commonplace household goods, giant trenches, silences, blank pieces of paper, and so forth, is to get people to regard aesthetically what they would not normally regard in this way (or perhaps even pay much attention to all), is to misunderstand entirely what many of these artists are after. For their avowed, often stridently proclaimed, intention is to make people abandon their usual habits of perception when confronted by something (to all intents and purposes) labelled 'art'.

Now if it is possible (as on some accounts it is) to adopt an aesthetic stance towards anything whatsoever, there will be no means of preventing someone from endeavouring to regard the various objects and performances in question from such a perspective if he is so inclined (or, as their authors might say, perverse or old-fashioned). We might bear in mind, too, that aesthetic aware-

[1] Cf. Wollheim, R., 'Minimal art', p. 107 (as reprinted in his *On Art and the Mind*).

ness can involve not only beauty and so on, but also ugliness, the grotesque, etc. However, in so far as the usual conventions to do with the way in which movement, paint, words, sounds and so forth are treated in art are missing, indeed deliberately flouted in anti-aesthetic pieces, an aesthetic response is in practice systematically rendered difficult. In contrast to *works*, conceived of as constructs or compositions, often with complex internal relations yielding several layers of meaning, and therefore demanding patience, skill, and imagination on the part of a 'distanced' contemplator, the *pieces* or *items* of many Post-Modern artists are not, it is held, to be regarded at all; rather, they are to be used, manipulated, entered into, interfered with, shared in, or even, in some instances, destroyed.

In other words such artists have sought to obliterate the distinction between an art object and any other sort of object in the physical world, denying that it is something more than physical (as postulated by aesthetic accounts) and placarding instead its 'thinghood'. It is just what it is, they assert (thereby begging the central question), available for instant apprehension without effort, experience or training on the part of anyone. Consequently professional performers may be dispensed with, members of a dance audience (say) being assigned everyday jobs and the resulting movements being designated the dance piece. The roles of critic and appreciator are also thus eliminated, since there is no longer any place, it is claimed, for interpretation, appraisal or assessment. As Mikel Dufrenne puts it in his Commentary on Elliott's 'The critic and the lover of art', the ('new') art object

> does not call the spectator to witness its perfection; it treats him rather as an accomplice or comrade, it invites him to take a more familiar attitude and also a more active part, it enlists his own creativity instead of his docility (p. 129).

Of course it might be suggested that before challenging others to examine their assumptions and prejudices about art, some Post-Modern artists should examine their own, perhaps in particular trying to gain a better understanding of the aesthetic. To imply, for example, that people sitting perfectly still and quiet are necessarily passive, docile, or inattentive as they watch or listen or read is as simple-minded as to suppose that so long as they are moving about or making noises they are necessarily actively engaged in art (or anything else). Again, it is quite erroneous to conclude that, since the concept of the aesthetic is tied historically to the concept of beauty, art created and appreciated from an aesthetic standpoint is merely decorative or 'other-worldly'.

Ideas to do with the 'otherness' of aesthetic experience are, indeed, especially liable to be misconstrued in connection with art. For the contrast of art with reality does not mean that art is thereby cut off from our experience of the everyday world and has no significance for day-to-day living (as I shall discuss further in later chapters). Moreover much of the widespread talk about the gap that is said to exist between life and art involves, as Wollheim points out, a confusion of a conceptual issue with one of a quite different kind, namely the practical problem of 'the many different devices, generally oppressively or enviously conceived, by which art has been segregated from those for whom it was made and turned into a preserve of the rich and the arrogant' (*On Art and the Mind*, p. 335).

Nevertheless while in recent years a number of dancers, painters, writers (and some of their apologists) have made mistakes such as these, it would be missing the point of what others have intended when they claim to be abolishing the distinction between art and reality if we were to suppose that what they were aiming at was to make art 'relevant' to ordinary life (whatever that might amount to). What exercises the minds of some of the more sophisticated is, rather, the issue of the *non-real* character of art, its imaginative or fictive or 'illusory' status (as postulated by many aesthetic accounts). Attempts to reduce the gap between art objects and physical objects have, of course, been familiar in the visual arts from the time of the Dadaists in the pre-1920s. But it is only with some Post-Modern pieces (including dances) that we see this aim all but realised, and the point almost reached at which, as Danto puts it, 'pure art collapses into pure reality' ('Artworks and real things', p. 4).

Yet it is not insignificant that, far from repudiating the title 'art' – unlike their early precursors who styled their work *anti-art* – Post-Modern artists wish specifically to retain it. This might be seen (as Osborne indicates in his paper, 'Aesthetic implications of conceptual art, happenings, etc.'), as nothing more than an attempt to attract to themselves something of the prestige that still attaches to the notion of fine art. But that (if true) is only part of the story: for such artists *not* to profess to be producing art would be entirely inconsistent with their aims, since it is with art that they are above all concerned. Or at least with ideas *about* art, its various instances functioning, so some claim, as *speech acts*[1], commenting, protesting, asserting, denying, joking, debunking, and so forth (more accurately in the case of the non-verbal arts, *quasi*-speech acts, Lyas observes: 'Danto and Dickie on art', p. 177).

Again, however, there is nothing new about art which serves as a vehicle for extolling or attacking ideas, events, states of affairs, etc. (several choreographers in the U.S.A., for example, have taken themes such as the Vietnam war, censorship of the arts, corruption in high places, and other issues prominent in American life in the 1960s and 1970s, as were comparable themes in the 1930s in Germany). Furthermore art has often been concerned with, and has com-

---

[1] A term made famous by J. L. Austin: see his *How to Do Things With Words*; also Searle, J. R., *Speech Acts: An Essay in the Philosophy of Language*.

mented on, its own traditions – not least, the illusion/reality issue; long before Samuel Beckett and Berthold Brecht, for instance, it was explored by Shakespeare in *A Midsummer Night's Dream*. And radical innovators from Picasso to Pirandello, from Stockhausen to Joyce, from Henry Moore to Martha Graham, have often set the critics, not to mention the general public, agog with the question, 'Can this really be art?' But what is different in the case of the artists we are now considering is that they deliberately set out to prompt the question, 'What *is* art?' – though it would seem to be going too far to claim, with Danto, that art itself has become its own *and only* subject matter ('Artworks and real things', p. 4), or with Binkley that

> extending and changing the concept 'art' is the business of art today, and not merely the by-product of the creative genius of a few people ('Deciding about art', p. 99).

A good deal of Post-Modern art then seems to be preoccupied with what has traditionally been the province of the philosopher – with questions to do with meaning and definition; with perception, imagination, and cognition; with the distinction between things as physical objects and things as symbols, between reality and appearance. However, instead of such problems being explored *within*, say, a novel, a dance, a play, as part of its subject matter – 'discussed' at one remove, as it were – they are instantiated in the object itself. Rather than thinking *about* them, as in a philosophy class or when reading a textbook, we are presented with them in concrete form, puzzled by the object or performance itself, perplexed as to how to take it.

Thus attempts are made in Post-Modern literature to upset the symbolising function of words and to give more than usual prominence to their physicality; movement as mere displacement of parts of the body is urged on the attention, so that any (e.g. purposeful or expressive) significance beyond that is thrown into question. By means such as constant repetition, unrelatedness, random-ness, and a variety of other 'dislocating' techniques, painted objects, move-ments, words and so forth are exhibited in such a way as to arouse doubt as regards their ontological status – what they 'really' are. Is this, for example, a real bed? Were those movements planned or spontaneous? Is this a genuine argument going on between the performers or not? And if someone is, say, following on-the-spot instructions to wade through mounds of wrapping paper and then tie a parcel,[1] is she *dancing* or merely the victim – or perpetrator – of a hoax? In other words, is this art or reality? Gene Blocker suggests:

[1] Cf. Cohen, S. J., *Dance as a Theatre Art*, p. 195.

> Like a Zen Koan, the distinction to be challenged is therapeutically pre-
> sented in a context where it becomes so difficult to keep the distinction
> straight, we soon tire of the effort and, momentarily at least, drop the
> distinction ('Autonomy, reference and Post-Modern art', p. 235).

But if, at the time, we are psychologically unfit to cope with the question, this
does not mean that it has gone away: it still remains a genuine problem for
philosophical reflection. Some Post-Modern artists, however, have seen
themselves as taking over from philosophers of art, naively supposing that if art,
like philosophy, is self-reflexive – that is, asks second-order questions about its
own nature – philosophy of art can be dispensed with altogether.[1] But, as Lyas
points out, there is an elementary error here. For the argument:

> Modern art is essentially second-order comment about art.
> Philosophy of art is essentially second-order comment about art.
>
> Ergo, Philosophy of art is modern art,
>
> is no more valid than:
>
> Dogs are animals.
> Cats are animals.
>
> Ergo, Cats are dogs
>
> ('Danto and Dickie on art', p. 235).

Moreover merely to *pose* a problem that has philosophical dimensions, or to
recognise one *as* philosophical, is hardly sufficient to qualify as 'doing philosophy'. Rather, an answer must be proposed, and if that answer is considered
wrong or inadequate, counter-arguments must be put forward and the
challenge accepted to pursue the debate in all its intricacy and complexity.
Needless to say, however, artists *qua* artists can hardly be expected to be up to
the task: their training does not fit them for it. Nor is it a matter of their trying
to find ever more novel or convincing ways in their work of closing more securely
the gap between art and reality. For the very attempt depends on the public's
assumption that there *is* just such a distinction: Post-Modern art inevitably
trades on the belief that art and reality are *not* one and the same thing.

For instance, for Marcel Duchamp's *Bicycle Wheel* of 1913 even to invite consideration as an art object it could not (as Blocker further notes) have been left
on an ordinary bicycle standing in a street, since then it would have failed to

---

[1] See, for example, Kosuth, J., 'Art after philosophy'.

make its 'point'. It could claim attention as art only because it was displayed in certain ways and circumstances, so that the very expectations it was intended to frustrate (or, alternatively perhaps, bring home to its viewers) could be taken for granted in the first place. It was just those circumstances and expectations – together, no doubt, with the fact that Duchamp was already an acknowledged artist – that predisposed people to regard the 'arrangement' (a bicycle wheel fixed upside down to a kitchen table) as art; they were what made its claim possible.

Precisely what Duchamp intended with his Readymades – whether, perhaps, he produced them for a variety of motives, some of which were in conflict – is a matter of some debate.[1] Diffey puts forward an interesting suggestion in 'On defining art' (by way of illustrating the general point that not everything of importance within the history of art is itself of artistic merit) that, by exemplifying the aesthetically nondescript, Readymades heighten our awareness of the values of what is already regarded as art. We are therefore not obliged, he argues, either to reject that art or to accept an item as an artwork simply because it makes a comment on art.

In any case it is clear that not all existing practices and conventions can be swept away by innovations in the arts. Quite the reverse: new instances of art stand in immediate need of at least some of those practices and conventions remaining unaltered, though these need not be the same ones in every case. There may or may not be, for example, permanent objects or repeatable performances; practices such as reviewing, buying and selling; aids such as pedestals, programme notes and catalogues (the latter often in fact of considerable importance for exhibitions and performances of Post-Modern art). Nevertheless the art 'piece' is always is *some* way treated differently from other things. Merely to be given a title or label is often of the greatest significance; for everyday sounds (or silences), objects such as urinals, movements such as conversational gestures or working actions, and the like, are in ordinary life precisely *not* labelled, say, *4 Minutes 33 Seconds*, *Fountain*, or *The Mind is a Muscle* (let alone *Trio* or *Street Dance*). Employing such devices is already to place the labelled item at a certain distance from the everyday world, however photographically similar it might be to the 'same' object or event in its usual context. Even to be called *Untitled* is to have a kind of title: as Danto remarks, what are not artworks are not entitled even to be untitled ('Artworks and real things', p. 11). Neither are these untitled objects, events, etc. discussed in art journals, taken from one place of performance or exhibition to another, or studied as part of the history of dance, painting, and so on.

It is also clear that the more radical the departure in art from what is already familiar and well-established, the greater is the dependence of each new arrival

---

[1] See, for example, Humble, P. N., 'Duchamp's Readymades: art and anti-art'.

on the existing art scene – the 'family' or 'world' of art objects – whose admirers not only are generally prepared to give a fair viewing or hearing to would-be entrants, but actually expect and even look for interesting, though perhaps initially disturbing or shocking developments. One might, of course, sympathise strongly with attempts to shake complacent audiences out of their typical attitudes, to bring art of all kinds to the masses in the street, the factory, the public house, the park, the village centre or the city square – places where 'ordinary' people are wont to congregate – and seek to stimulate their curiosity and active participation. One might also warmly approve efforts in the performing arts to challenge the cult of personality. But revolutionaries (and would-be revolutionaries) in the arts merely deceive themselves if they imagine that what they are doing, or trying to do, is immediately obvious or intelligible to everyone. Far from having instant appeal or being readily accepted as art by the vast majority, *avant-garde* works (like *avant-garde* ideas in the sciences or elsewhere, which seem calculated to upset established practice and theory) can have only a limited impact, and then usually on those already on the inside of the activity in question. The early audiences of Post-Modern dance in Greenwich Village, for instance, were themselves artists and intellectuals – audiences, as Sally Banes mentions, 'acutely aware of the crises in modern art and knowledgeable about the history of alternatives to art traditions, eager to be surprised, shocked, provoked' (*Terpsichore in Sneakers*, p. 13).

The gap between art and reality, however, can never be completely closed; for in that case we should have no need of the concept of art at all. If art just *were* reality it would be simply, as Danto has to admit, 'a roundabout way of getting at what we already *have*' (p. 4). Although some instances of art superficially resemble everyday objects and activities, then, the fact that we normally treat them differently, feel and think about them differently from, say, gasworks, burglar alarms or the movements we use each day while dressing, indicates that artworks occupy a role in our lives to be contrasted, not identified, with these other things and pursuits. We do, that is, *operate* with a concept of art: it is (as discussed in the previous chapter), a regulative concept in our lives.

Nevertheless it does not follow from this that art necessarily involves *aesthetic* appreciation; and rather than focusing on accounts in which, say, disinterested contemplation is of central importance to an understanding of the concept of art, it is evident that we have to examine the social and historical framework within which the concept sits. To repeat a point stressed earlier: any attempt to characterise art in terms of something *additional* to the rest of a society's practices and habits of thought and feeling, let alone unconnected with them, is totally misdirected.

More remains to be said, however, about the role of imagination in our experience of a good many artworks and the resemblance (or otherwise) between such experience and the way in which we sometimes appreciate, say, natural phenomena or sporting activities. For the relationship between art and the aesthetic has so far been discussed chiefly from the point of view of whether the aesthetic is a necessary feature of art. What has not yet been considered is whether it is, rather, the notion of art that is logically prior to that of the aesthetic. It might, for example, be proposed that when we take an aesthetic interest in something which is *not* art, we nevertheless regard it as if it were. But this, as Beardsmore points out in 'Two trends in contemporary aesthetics', is a somewhat ambiguous suggestion: if the claim is that in order to treat a piece of driftwood or a game of cricket as art we must already possess the concept of art, this amounts to a rather unedifying tautology. On the other hand the proposal might be that an aesthetic interest in things is possible only in a society in which artistic activities are carried on – a thesis strongly argued by Wollheim in *Art and Its Objects*.

On this view, rather than our experience of art being one variety of a kind of experience that is understood primarily by reference to non-art phenomena – perhaps, in particular, natural beauty – aesthetic appreciation of such phenomena is, on the contrary, an extension of an attitude or disposition that is understood primarily by reference to artworks. In other words, Wollheim insists, artworks constitute paradigm or central cases of aesthetic appreciation, while natural phenomena, etc. are peripheral or borderline cases.

Now it would certainly seem mistaken, as Beardsmore argues, to suppose that appreciation of art (or, at any rate, much art) is to be understood simply as a more sophisticated or complicated version of our admiration of the beauty of a rose or our experience of certain things seen and heard during a fog at sea, such as is vividly described by Edward Bullough in his paper, ' "Psychical distance" as a factor in art and an aesthetic principle'. But it was no part of Bullough's purpose, Beardsmore suggests, to claim that such experiences are *paradigms* of artistic appreciation: rather, he was concerned with the appreciation of nature as having important affinities with experience of art, and with how such appreciation might throw light on art experience. Moreover it is equally mistaken, Beardsmore maintains, to suppose that the aesthetic enjoyment of roses, toadstools, jellyfish and much more can ever adequately be understood if we think primarily in terms of our experience of sculptures, paintings and so forth. That is, to give an account of the *aesthetic* in terms of *art* is no less disadvantageous for an understanding of the aesthetic than is the reverse procedure for an understanding of art. It therefore seems to me that Beardsmore is right to conclude that the two concepts are best regarded as logically independent.

This is not, however, to deny that there are strong contingent connections between the two; nor that many artworks – perhaps most – are still produced and appraised under the concept of the aesthetic, despite the fact (or what appears to be the fact) that at the present time the concept of imagination as central to art is giving way to something else – though what, precisely, is not yet clear. In view then of the continuing importance for much art criticism of what are often claimed to be aesthetic qualities, and yet at the same time a widespread confusion as to how these are to be characterised, it is to this problem that we must now turn.

CHAPTER SIX

Aesthetic qualities: The 'objectivist' account

> We find certain things about seeing puzzling because we do not find the whole business of seeing puzzling enough.
>
> L. Wittgenstein: *Philosophical Investigations*

It might generally be agreed that a notable feature of the arts during the present century has been an ever-increasing concern with the medium itself. In music, of course, by the very nature of things, this concern has always been pre-eminent, whereas in those arts in which reference to matters that are external to the medium is possible (and indeed in almost all literature and drama, unavoidable[1]), the importance of formal qualities, qualities of rhythm, design, structure, etc., may vary from one work to another.

This is nowhere more evident than in the dance, which in this respect stands somewhere between music at one extreme and narrative literature at the other. For while the dance can, and frequently does, deal with events and situations of the outside world, particularly of human existence, it can also, despite the ineradicable overtones of expressiveness in bodily gesture and bearing, approximate very closely to music in its freedom from referential meaning. It is therefore hardly surprising that, in keeping with trends in other art forms, a major interest of much theatre dance in recent years, as well as of many historical and folk dances as we know them, lies not in the story line or some 'message', but in the qualities and configurations of movement itself. Some choreographers, indeed (as, for example, some of those contributing to Cohen's *The Modern Dance*), claim that this is *all* that matters, though such features of course play a crucial role also in representational works in the depicting of character, mood, and so forth.

In a good deal of writing on the dance, however, the terms 'quality', 'qualities', 'movement qualities', etc. are apt to be used in a variety of ways; and, perhaps because the dancing person rather than his movement is often (erroneously) thought of as the medium of the dance, talk about quality and qualities tends to be confused, especially when it goes hand in hand with talk about the *experience* of the performer. Sometimes then mention of quality has to do with the physical sensations of, for instance, flying through the air, folding or

---

[1] Exceptions are 'sound poems', such as those of Kurt Schwitters, in which no conventional words are used.

unfolding the limbs, or stamping vigorously – experience that is often mistaken for aesthetic experience. Sometimes it has to do with what is alleged to be psychosomatic experience of a special and complex kind, the mover's whole being, it is claimed, feeling light, timeless, expansive, and such like[1] – thus giving rise to a host of problems both of meaning and verification. And sometimes it involves obscure references, typically shrouded in vague, if not meaningless, metaphysical language, to *inner* quality, *inner* experience, the *inner* significance of movement, and so on. Erick Hawkins, for example, writes:

> the important essence of all dancing is *movement quality* . . . the wondrous, immediate knowledge of existence that you get in the pure fact of movement can come only if you find that inner quality . . . . Pure movement is decorative, instead of significant, if the inner quality is lacking ('Pure poetry', p. 39).

Yet whether there is talk of 'innerness' or not, of movement quality in general or of particular movement or dance qualities, it usually seems to be assumed by the speaker that what he is referring to is available for others besides himself to perceive. Thus there is rarely any hesitation on the part of those who claim to have 'immediate knowledge' to point out to the less discerning when, say, movement is delicate as distinct from relaxed, urgent or excited as distinct from merely fast or vigorous. That is, such qualities are held to be publicly observable, even if not straightforwardly so. And certainly, should one person fail to see or hear in an artwork or a performance qualities that another claims *he* can see or hear, or, alternatively, claim to perceive something different, it does not necessarily follow that the experience in question is private or unshareable, nor that statements involving reference to such qualities are beyond rational discussion and incapable of justification (or refutation).

Nevertheless it does seem that the perception of qualities such as delicacy or robustness differs in some way from that of, for instance, the tempo of a dance, its dotted rhythms, or its mainly circular floor patterns. Similarly with, say, the solemnity or joyousness of a piece of music on the one hand, and, on the other, its metre or loudness or pitch. Even those qualities of a person's physical appearance known variously as 'expressive', 'feeling', 'affective', or (chiefly in psychology) 'physiognomic' qualities seem to require different means of establishing objectivity from that appropriate in the case of features such as the shade of his hair, his height, weight, and so forth. Those qualities in virtue of which we ascribe to people particular moods, emotions, attitudes, etc. seem, it is true, to be inherent in the pattern we perceive, not something additional to it: we apprehend them directly, not by a process of inference (e.g., her brow is

[1] See, for example, Laban, R., *Mastery of Movement*, pp. 74–85.

furrowed, she is pacing up and down: *therefore*, she must be anxious). Yet the same bodily posture, gesture or 'arrangement' of facial features can, when seen in different contexts, take on very varied expressions. Wittgenstein writes:

> I see a picture which represents a smiling face. What do I do if I take the smile now as a kind one, now as malicious? Don't I often imagine it with a spatial and temporal context which is one either of kindness or malice? Thus I might supply the picture with the fancy that the smiler was smiling down on a child at play, or again on the suffering of an enemy (*Philosophical Investigations*, para. 539).

This is the sort of consideration that presumably inspired the experiment in film montage reported by Michael Chanan in which the close-up of an actor who adopted a completely impassive facial expression was undercut with, first, a bowl of soup, then a young woman lying dead in her coffin, and finally a child playing with a teddy-bear. The result was that the audience described the actor as looking *pensively* at the bowl of soup, *sorrowfully* at the coffin, and *smilingly* at the child ('Art and experiment', p. 139). Further, as Isabel Hungerland points out in her paper, 'Once again, aesthetic and non-aesthetic', no court of law would accept as a proper basis for identifying a suspect the testimony of any number of witnesses who were agreed about the expressive qualities of his general mien and movements.

Sometimes too there are what seem to be puzzling discrepancies between the two sorts of quality in question. A dancer, for example, may *appear* to float effortlessly off the ground and to weigh scarcely anything at all as he soars airily upward, though he *actually* exerts a good deal of force and maintains considerable tension throughout his body as he does so; another with quite lazy-looking movement may nevertheless progress across a stage at a faster rate than one whose movement has a more hurried, energetic quality.

What then is the logical status of those qualities that seem so vividly to be present, often persisting in the face of evidence to the contrary, yet that may change as we look (or listen) again, perhaps when we notice further features of the movement (or sound, etc.), so that what initially struck us as, say, diffuse or rambling now seems economical and perfectly integrated? In other words, how do such qualities differ from, and how are they related to, properties to do with shape, size, pitch, colour, and so on? Are they 'really' there, or not?

We have already had occasion to note that throughout the history of aesthetic enquiry similar questions have arisen in the particular case of beauty, grace, ugliness, and the like – qualities often assumed to be specifically *aesthetic*. Nor are such questions of merely academic interest, something for theorists to speculate about in moments of idle curiosity. For reference to such qualities, often alongside reference to more straightforwardly observable properties, usually plays an important role in critical debate, especially in connection with the evaluation of artworks and the justification of aesthetic appraisals (indeed the term 'aesthetic qualities' is sometimes used to mean those qualities in virtue of which an object is judged aesthetically good or bad – by some, *artistically* good or bad). It also features extensively in the teaching and rehearsal situations, where individuals who normally recognise without difficulty, say, movement that is straight or jerky or slow, and sounds that are quiet or loud, low-pitched or high, are not always able to pick out a dance or a musical performance that is, for instance, fiery or spirited (not merely quick), dynamic (not merely correctly phrased and accented), or austere (not merely controlled and precise); nor, further, to discern a work that has well-developed motifs or a disproportionately long introduction, that is fragmented or well rounded-off; nor, while observing that two dancers are near together on one side of the stage, are unaware of their being *too close* together or *too far* over to one side, and are insensitive to the resulting imbalance and loss of dramatic power.

The earlier question about beauty and its cognates is, in fact, but one aspect of a much wider and long-standing philosophical enquiry about knowledge and the nature of reality: about what we can know of the external world, what sort of characteristics, if any, are possessed by things independently of our perception of them, what sort depend on certain capacities and sensibilities of the perceiver, what sort require more than ordinary sense perception, and so forth. The question is thus part of an enquiry involving complex issues to do with substance, mind, perception and, not least, language. It is nevertheless sometimes mistakenly assumed to be a question for psychology. But although there are, of course, many psychological problems that arise here, no piece of empirical research can help us with the main task in hand at the moment, namely how to identify and characterise *aesthetic* qualities. For how such qualities are to be distinguished from other sorts cannot be separated from the question of how aesthetic appraisals are to be justified: problems about perception are always tied to problems to do with knowledge claims, criteria and evidence.

We might begin by getting a few linguistic difficulties out of the way; for a variety of labels attaches to those qualities for which there are no standardised tests for normal observers in normal conditions. Sometimes, for example, they are known as 'second-order' or 'emergent' qualities, sometimes as 'tertiary' or 'field' or 'Gestalt' qualities. 'Emergent' indicates the idea of their alleged emergence from, or some kind of dependence on, what in turn are variously referred to as 'first-order', 'objective', 'physical' or 'observable' properties. 'Tertiary' derives from John Locke's controversial distinction[1] in Book II of the

---

[1] This distinction in fact goes back much further to the fifth century B.C. and was revived by Galileo, Descartes, Boyle, and Newton, among others; but it was Locke who gave it its classical formulation. For a useful discussion of qualities, properties, etc. see Hospers, J., *An Introduction to Philosophical Analysis*, p. 499ff.

Essay Concerning Human Understanding between what he designated *primary* qualities (qualities, for instance, of a thing's size, weight or shape), and *secondary* qualities (its colour, sound, taste, etc.). The terms 'field' and 'Gestalt' reflect the interest of the Gestalt school of psychology in what seems to be a natural human disposition to organise, say, a collection of dots or a sequence of sounds into coherent wholes, so that what is perceived is a pattern, a melody, and such like. Perhaps then since it avoids the need to subscribe unreservedly to the complex theories associated with either 'tertiary' or 'Gestalt', the term *second-order* qualities is least problematic, though it must not, of course, be confused with Locke's idea of secondary qualities. Neither should it be taken as indicating qualities in any way inferior to, or less important than, those features for which there are standard tests of verification, and which I shall call *first-order* features (or qualities, characteristics, etc.).

Now as regards aesthetic awareness, a question arises immediately in the case of that sub-group of (second-order) qualities referred to a moment ago as 'expressive' or 'physiognomic'. These qualities, we may note, are commonly attributed not only to human beings, and hence, understandably, to dances, plays, films, and operas, but also to inanimate phenomena: we speak of jolly tunes, serene landscapes, noble buildings, majestic mountains; of the sprightly rhythms of a poem, the sombre colours of a painting, and so on. Yet there seems no reason to claim that our perception of everyday mood and feeling in the physical appearance of people always, or even often, coincides with an *aesthetic* interest in such appearances. Notwithstanding Hungerland's remarks on aesthetic and non-aesthetic qualities in the paper referred to above, to perceive the angry or cheerful look of a face hardly seems adequate to warrant claims about perceiving aesthetically. Indeed it is usually in the course of our day-to-day communication and dealings with people that we take note of, for example, a gloomy or perplexed facial expression, a buoyant step, a dignified stance, or a dejected posture – during, that is, the conduct of practical and moral affairs; and such recognition is to be contrasted, rather than identified, with aesthetic awareness.

If then some second-order qualities are only sometimes aesthetic, wherein, it might be asked, lies the difference? We might do better, however, to pose the question in another way, to ask: 'What *makes* them aesthetic?' Or, more strictly, 'Under what (logical) conditions do they, or other qualities, *count* as aesthetic?' Such a reformulation of the original question leads, as might be anticipated from what was said in the previous chapter, to the suggestion that aesthetic awareness is not a matter of discovering a particular kind of quality *in* things, but involves rather a special mode of attention, a special attitude or stance on the part of the experiencing individual.

It need hardly be said that how to characterise such an attitude or stance remains a major problem. Nevertheless such an approach is widely regarded as potentially fruitful. But it is as well to be aware that some contemporary philosophers continue to adhere to the notion of distinctively aesthetic qualities and concepts, as contrasted with non-aesthetic qualities and concepts, although (predictably) accounts of how the alleged distinction is to be drawn vary considerably. It is therefore important to understand why, whatever the details of any such account, attempting to tackle the problem from this angle might be thought mistaken; and why, even if a wholly satisfactory analysis of aesthetic interest may still elude us, a 'point of view' or 'mode of attention' approach is, in principle, to be preferred.

In the first place, it should be noted that theories based on the idea of there being specifically aesthetic concepts which apply to features of objects – and hence known, rather confusingly perhaps, as *objectivist* theories – construe aesthetic appraisals as little more than special cases of 'pure' description, rather than as involving interpretative and evaluative elements. Aesthetic qualities are 'there' to be perceived somewhat after the manner of a thing's size or shape or colour – though a qualification is usually entered here about specially 'competent' or 'sensitive' observers. Claims about aesthetic qualities are thus held to be true or false in the way that perceptual claims are true or false. In other words (though it may not always be obvious) aesthetic appreciation is characterised as a species of *knowledge that* such and such is the case. These theories are therefore also known, again rather confusingly in view of the everyday use of the term 'cognition', as *cognitive* theories (i.e. involving the notion of belief).

Accounts which, by contrast, take an 'attitude' or 'mode of attention' approach of some sort regard aesthetic appraisals as having an inescapably personal aspect, with a marked evaluative element (though this is not to deny that some may carry strongly descriptive suggestions: 'pretty', for example, indicates something small, slight and neat, not large or substantial[1]). We see an object *as* lovely (grotesque, etc.) rather than *recognising* loveliness as we recognise, say, redness or roundness. Such theories, sometimes known as *subjectivist* theories, thus allow the possibility of two – or more – logically incompatible claims being equally defensible: they are not so much true or false as appropriate or inappropriate, apt or idiosyncratic, reasonable or unreasonable. This will be discussed further in the next chapter, which will argue for a particular version of an 'attitude' approach to the question of aesthetic interest.

A notable example of the first kind of account, i.e. the objectivist or cognitivist kind, has been furnished by F. N. Sibley, who has been concerned in a series of papers dating from 1959 with the nature of what he proposes are aesthetic, as

[1] For a fuller discussion of this point, with particular reference to the dance, see my 'Aesthetic qualities in the dance and their significance in education', p. 219ff.

distinct from non-aesthetic, concepts. His position is perhaps most explicitly stated in 'Aesthetic qualities and the looks of things' (published shortly after, though not as widely discussed as, his seminal paper, 'Aesthetic concepts'). Here, after entertaining briefly the idea that it might be 'not so much *what* as *how* we notice that makes our attention aesthetic', Sibley goes on to assert that it is quite mistaken to suppose that 'by simply changing to an aesthetic approach or "contemplation", we can value or admire for itself any quality or appearance'.[1] In a more recent paper, 'Particularity, art and evaluation', he further maintains that terms such as *elegant, graceful, ungainly, hideous* 'indicate the presence of a particular property' and are thus used in a neutral or descriptive way – even if it happens that the quality in question is widely valued (or disvalued); similarly, that terms such as *balanced, evocative, witty, moving* (all aesthetic terms on Sibley's account), 'fall fairly clearly into the descriptive category and could be applied by someone who did not value such qualities' (p. 8): they apply, it seems, to features *recognised, found in* things. Then again, in 'Aesthetic concepts', a sharp distinction between describing and interpreting is evident when Sibley claims that there are a good many artworks, as well as such things as buildings, furniture, faces and scenery, about which questions of interpretation do not arise at all.

Now the concept of interpretation is one of considerable complexity, not least in the case of art, with additional ramifications in the case of the performing arts. For instance, there is the kind which construes, say, Martha Graham's *Acrobats of God* as a skit on the dancing profession, or Hindemith's *Mathis der Maler* as a gesture of defiance against the Nazis; and it is this sort (Beardsley, in *The Possibility of Criticism*, labels them 'superimpositions'), that presumably Sibley has in mind here. But to speak of a cathedral or a landscape as *tranquil* or *sombre*, let alone a dance or some other work of art as *tragic, sentimental, trite* or *powerful* (more of Sibley's aesthetic terms) can hardly be thought straightforwardly descriptive – if, indeed, the idea of pure or straightforward description is tenable at all. On the contrary, such terms are strongly interpretative. Moreover interpretations of the first kind ('superimpositions') do not seem completely separable from the second. To see *Acrobats of God* as a send-up of the dancing profession, for example, is also to see it as a light-hearted, witty, playful dance, not as, say, harrowing or stark: a different construal (interpretation$_1$) would go hand in hand with seeing different aesthetic qualities (interpretation$_2$).

It is by means of an impressive array of terms and expressions such as those just instanced, as contrasted with another, allegedly non-aesthetic set, that (in

---

[1] p. 341 as reprinted in (ed.) F. J. Coleman, *Contemporary Studies in Aesthetics* (page numbers throughout refer to this volume).

'Aesthetic concepts') Sibley introduces his thesis – though he adds in a footnote what I shall later suggest is a very important qualification, and one to which far greater significance should be attached than he appears to allow, namely that it would be more correct to speak of their *use* as aesthetic or non-aesthetic terms. But although how someone refers to an object or performance is certainly one of the chief means by which we may seek to establish whether or not his interest in it is aesthetic (as we shall have occasion to consider further in Chapter 8), what requires examination here is how, on Sibley's view, the contrast is to be upheld.

The basis of the division between his two groups of remarks is that the aesthetic kind involves 'the exercise of taste, perceptiveness, or sensitivity, of aesthetic discrimination or appreciation',[1] *taste* here meaning not likes or dislikes, matters of merely fashionable, social or personal preferences (and hence philosophically uninteresting), but 'an ability to *notice* or *see* or *tell* that things have certain qualities' (p. 66). Someone so equipped is, then, able to perceive that an artwork holds together, lacks balance, or has a certain repose; that something is vivid, delicate, lifeless, etc. Examples of Sibley's non-aesthetic remarks are that a work has a great many characters (as against 'there are too many characters'); that there is a reconciliation scene in the fifth act; or that something is square, noisy or evanescent. And these observations, Sibley claims, do *not* require the exercise of any special ability or training, but could be made by anyone with normal eyes, ears and intelligence (and, Meager pertinently adds in *her* paper, 'Aesthetic concepts', with a command of language).

Nevertheless the two sorts of quality are related, Sibley argues, in that the former *result* or *emerge* from, are *due* to the latter: something is, for example, graceful *on account of* its lines or movements, whereas something red does not depend in a similar way on any of its other perceptible qualities.[2] However, the peculiar logic of aesthetic concepts, Sibley goes on to maintain, is that they are in no way rule-governed or conditional upon non-aesthetic concepts: no collection of the latter can ever provide logically sufficient conditions for the application of aesthetic terms. We cannot, that is, infer or reason from the fact, say, that a dance is in a quick tempo and consists predominantly of light skips and jumps, etc. that it is gay and cheerful. Hence, according to Sibley, the need for 'taste' – and it is perhaps not insignificant that he uses here a term that almost inevitably carries overtones of eighteenth-century aesthetic theory.

Everything turns therefore on this notion. But his account immediately faces the danger of circularity: aesthetic qualities are qualities requiring the exercise of taste, taste consists in the discrimination of aesthetic qualities. Sibley has also frequently been accused of postulating the existence of some mysterious mental

[1] p. 64, as reprinted in (ed.) J. Margolis, *Philosophy Looks at the Arts*, 2nd edn. (page numbers throughout refer to this volume).
[2] Cf. Sibley's 'Aesthetic concepts: a rejoinder', p. 81.

faculty or sixth sense, thus adopting an intuitionist position in aesthetics similar to that sometimes found in ethics (most notably in G. E. Moore's *Principia Ethica*), namely of supposing that, although certain qualities are not given to sense perception, they are nevertheless apprehended, or intuited, directly as properties of things, actions, etc.

What is needed then to meet these charges is further elaboration of the idea of the special sort of sensitivity or perceptiveness that Sibley talks about, and of what he means when he says in another paper, 'Aesthetic and non-aesthetic', that 'aesthetics deals with a kind of perception' (p. 137). He is, of course, quite right to insist that in the aesthetic situation there must be firsthand experience of whatever is in question, that 'people have to *see* the grace or unity of a work, *hear* the plaintiveness or frenzy in the music, *notice* the gaudiness of a colour scheme, *feel* the power of a novel, its mood, or its uncertainty of tone'. But when it comes to the question of how such appraisals are to be justified, how this alleged 'perceptiveness' is to be checked for accuracy, it appears that, with some adaptation, the model is to be that employed in settling claims about colour: there has to be 'a certain kind of appeal to agreement in reaction or discrimination', those individuals with the most detailed discrimination being taken as setting the standards ('Objectivity and aesthetics', p. 36).

It follows therefore that someone is either right or wrong in a particular case (though since there is no entailment relation between a remark containing a non-aesthetic term and one containing an aesthetic term, he cannot of course be shown to be *logically* correct or incorrect). Sibley's account thus does not allow for the possibility of the same set of non-aesthetic features 'yielding' different aesthetic qualities; or, to put the point another way, conflicting aesthetic appraisals cannot, on this view, be equally defensible – as, however, is possible if they are regarded not as perceptual claims, but as interpretations.[1] Yet in 'Objectivity and aesthetics' Sibley concedes that some aesthetic ascriptions are better considered as reasonable or unreasonable, admissible or inadmissible, and so forth, than as right or wrong, true or false. But this, as Margolis suggests in his paper, 'Robust relativism', seems to indicate a move towards a relativist position (such as he himself favours, as does Michael Tanner in his reply to 'Objectivity and aesthetics').

What is nevertheless important to note here is that all three writers share a similar conception of objectivity, namely one that requires a large measure of *actual* agreement – even though this may, according to Sibley, be found only among an (in this case, aesthetic) élite. Moreover while it is clear that there is a great variety of remarks ranging from the more straightforwardly descriptive or informative to those that involve a considerable degree of interpretation, it

---

[1] This is convincingly illustrated and the whole subject well discussed by Roger Scruton in his *Art and Imagination*, ch. 3.

would be mistaken to suppose that this range is one only of degree and not of kind. For the various modes by which we structure our experience (e.g. scientific, moral, aesthetic), involve different ways of establishing objectivity: they are susceptible to different kinds of 'test'. For Sibley to speak then of a gradual transition in aesthetic remarks from true to apt description, and to claim (as in his contribution to a Symposium, 'About taste'), that there is a range 'from the more to the less typically objective' would seem to deny or at least to overlook the possiblity that, rather than sometimes approximating to, but often falling short of 'real' objectivity, aesthetic appraisals demand their own sort of justification – a different application of reasoning altogether.

The suggestion that aesthetic qualities are qualities of the sort that admit of verification procedures such as are appropriate in, say, the case of colour discrimination, for which standard conditions and standard observers can be specified, thus claims objectivity for aesthetic appreciation in a way that reduces it to something else. It is to assume that, as with ordinary sense perception, what is involved are mental states and activities related to believing, information-seeking, and the like; whereas in aesthetic awareness it would seem that certain mental powers – in particular those of imagination and feeling – are differently employed (in a way yet to be explicated). For when we experience something aesthetically, whether it be a ballet or a cherry tree in blossom or a star-studded sky, we are not concerned with the recognition of certain features of the object or activity, as would be the case if we took, say, a biological or botanical or astronomical interest, but rather with how it *strikes* or *impresses* us. In ascribing aesthetic qualities to something, we are indicating, perhaps even, it might be said, *expressing* our attitude towards it.

Thus to see a dance as dreary or hilarious, as creating a mysterious atmosphere or having a haunting loveliness, is not like noticing that it was accompanied by gongs and bells or made use of different levels by means of ramps, though of course we do have to be able to perceive details such as these (indeed, which ones we actually notice, together with other sorts of knowledge we may have, can make a significant difference to our response). Aesthetic ascriptions then testify to our awareness of a dance (or whatever it might be) as having some feeling tone, as being invested with some personal significance – often, though not necessarily, significance of a profound or disturbing kind. Any account of aesthetic qualities that leaves out all mention of the experienced response of the percipient is therefore, I shall maintain, inadequate. For such perception-centred accounts underplay the importance of the individual's imaginative and emotional powers of response.[1] If, indeed, cognitive theories were correct, aesthetic appraisals would be nothing more – and nothing less –

[1] This is well argued by Meager in 'Aesthetic concepts'; see also Elliott, R. K., 'Aesthetic theory and the experience of art' and his 'Imagination in the experience of art'.

than a species of judgment subject to verification or falsification after the manner of ordinary perceptual claims. In consequence, none of the lively controversy and interest in other people's views characteristically generated by works of art, dress, townscapes and so on would ever occur; neither would there be any occasion for sharing or challenging the responses of others, or for gaining from them insights we might otherwise not have had. As Schaper observes, if beauty (say) *were* straightforwardly a quality in objects, no one need bother about it particularly or take delight in pointing it out; trying to establish objectivity in the way in which ordinary perceptual claims are established 'would be the worst sin we could commit against those experiences that give rise to judgments of taste'.[1]

This does not mean, however, that aesthetic awareness is independent of perceptual experience. On the contrary, in seeking to give an account that does justice both to the personal response of the experiencing individual *and* to the object of his attention, it is possible to start with those (first-order) properties of an object or activity for which there are standard tests of verification, and characterise aesthetic qualities in terms of a particular way of attending to those properties – in terms, that is, of *how* rather than *what* we perceive. Thus features of things such as their shapes or colours or movement attributes, whether of natural phenomena or man-made objects, whether artworks or otherwise, are regarded *under a particular description*.

How more precisely this is to be understood is the subject of the next chapter; but what may be pointed out at once is that on this view it follows that there can be no restriction on what might be the object of aesthetic interest. Anything may, in principle, become the focus – though in practice it might be difficult: as Strawson suggests, 'It would be very precious for anyone to say that he found predication or disjunction aesthetically admirable . . . .' ('Aesthetic appraisal and works of art', p. 179). The possibility mentioned earlier of second-order qualities *coming* to count as aesthetic is thus extended to *any* property. This may not be an easy idea to entertain initially; but it should be borne in mind, first, that it is a *formal* requirement, and secondly, that an aesthetic stance may involve an *un*favourable response.

The emphasis shifts then from exclusive consideration of the object of attention to consideration of the mode in which that object is attended to; from a concern with a type of property to concern with the mental state or activity of the experiencing person, as made evident in a certain kind of response and a manner of reasoning by which such a response may be justified. Instead of

---

[1] *Studies in Kant's Aesthetics*, p. 76. (The term 'taste' is used here within the Kantian idiom and does not commit Schaper to Sibley's thesis; 'judgments of taste' may be taken as the equivalent of 'aesthetic appraisals'.)

attempting to mark off a set of peculiarly aesthetic objects or qualities, we move over to the view that there is, as Meager puts it, an 'infinite elasticity of the class of *possibly* aesthetically forceful features' ('Aesthetic concepts, p. 308). It is not so much that, for example, pale colours or tapering fingers or soft sounds might *explain* the delicacy of something; rather they *constitute* it. In the case of a dance, therefore, it is just *that* particular organisation of steps and gestures, rhythms, group formations and the like which constitute, say, its thrilling climax or its tame introduction, its tightly-knit character or its jarring disjointedness.

The nature of the relationship between the aesthetic and the non-aesthetic is thus one, not of entailment (as Sibley rightly insists), but of presupposition: aesthetic, as contrasted with normal (or what Scruton calls 'literal'[1]) attention, presupposes knowledge of what is the case. Correspondingly, what is typical of a great deal of discussion in the aesthetic realm is that we borrow language from a variety of other spheres and, as Schaper expresses it, transpose it into a different key (*Prelude to Aesthetics*, pp. 15–16). With the exception of that small group of words and phrases that usually have specifically aesthetic force, the terms employed thus have a 'detached' or 'fluid' character, deriving their meaning from a non-aesthetic use and therefore requiring in the first place an understanding of that use.[2] Somewhat as the everyday context of the *object* is left behind when it is regarded aesthetically, yet remains as a kind of backcloth, so in *talk* about it words retain their normal meanings, but, in coming to have a special (aesthetic) use, they contribute to a new realm of discourse, logically distinct, yet not unrelated to other realms.

While then it may be useful to speak of 'aesthetic qualities' as short for 'qualities regarded aesthetically', we should beware that this is apt to reinforce the idea that there are qualities of a distinctively aesthetic kind; and, rather than speak of 'aesthetic concepts', which may suggest that certain words and phrases have one, and only one, correct usage (i.e. aesthetic), we should, strictly, speak of *concepts functioning aesthetically* – that is, in adverbial, rather than in adjectival, terms (cf. Schaper's *Studies in Kant's Aesthetics*, p. 119). Similarly 'aesthetic perception' can be an ambiguous and misleading expression; but again, as long as it is used and understood to refer to *a way of regarding* something, not to the perception of something peculiarly aesthetic, no harm need be done.

The question now arises, however, as to whether aesthetic awareness depends *only* on information available to the senses. It comes to the fore chiefly (though Hepburn considers here some interesting examples of natural phenomena[3]) in connection with art and art criticism; for a good deal of information of a non-

---

[1] *The Aesthetics of Architecture*, ch. 4. (This is an excellent discussion of the subject.)

[2] Cf. Scruton, R., op. cit., p. 234; also his *Art and Imagination*, ch. 4.

[3] 'Contemporary aesthetics and the neglect of natural beauty', p. 295 ff.

perceptual kind is clearly necessary for the appreciation of many artworks. Someone ignorant of the political, religious, and symbolic aspects of Picasso's *Guernica*, for example, or of Christopher Bruce's *Cruel Garden*, and the life of Federico Garcia Lorca on which the latter is based, would miss much of the power, subtlety, and pathos of these works. Moreover what may also be a vital ingredient of the appreciator's 'cognitive stock', as Wollheim aptly calls it, is an understanding of the artistic traditions from which a work derives, the cultural conventions of certain art forms, and the categories of genre, style, representation and so on that are employed in art discourse. Without such knowledge and some grasp of what the artist regarded himself as doing – his intentions and expectations in producing a work (or 'piece') and the general beliefs, technological innovations, etc. against which those intentions and expectations were formed – we might well approach that work quite inappropriately (*Art and Its Objects*, p. 194 ff.).

Those who warn against the 'intentional fallacy', therefore, arguing that we should ignore all information about the origins of a work and the background of the artist in order to concentrate on *the work itself*, are begging the very question at issue. Of course a good many biographical details and other information about the genesis of a work may be completely irrelevant to appreciation; but many that *are* relevant, indeed vital, are far from straightforwardly observable.

The problem is further complicated when, as with Beardsley, for example, an artwork is taken to consist exclusively of its aesthetic qualities. After trying for many years to define the aesthetic, and thence art, in terms of a special kind of perceptual awareness, Beardsley does not, it is true, advance an objectivist theory of the kind proposed by Sibley. Rather, his is a sort of 'attitude' account, though one that does not, so to speak, hand over complete responsibility to the individual for his aesthetic experiences. Nevertheless the adopting of an aesthetic stance seems, on this view, to be the means whereby access is gained to a particular kind of quality *in* things: provided that the percipient 'switches on' the appropriate kind of attention, what becomes available to him is objectively there.

More recently, as in his paper 'The aesthetic point of view', Beardsley has taken to speaking of experiencing, rather than perceiving, aesthetic qualities; and, further, builds into his account reference to their effect on the person, namely in terms of a species of gratification. But for Beardsley a work of art remains identified with its aesthetic qualities: they make up, in his terminology, *the aesthetic object* – something set over against, existing alongside, the physical object, or that which, as he puts it, 'consists of things and events describable in the language of physics' (*Aesthetics*, p. 31). It is not surprising, therefore, that he should see the aims and functions of the critic as involving true statements about the merits of artworks and informing people, i.e. imparting *facts*, accordingly: 'there is a proximate end in judging', he says, 'namely, to provide information about value' (*The Possibility of Criticism*, pp. 63–64).

Beardsley was, it may be noted, co-author of the celebrated paper (first published in 1946), 'The intentional fallacy', which, despite its title, does not limit discussion to the intentions of the artist, but extends to considerations of other aspects of a work's history. In treating artworks as self-enclosed entities, fully open to direct inspection, Beardsley thus rules out the possible relevance for appreciation of any factors external to 'the work itself' – the aesthetic object.[1]

According to this view then it makes no difference to our response to a work whether or not we know, for example, that it was inspired (if that is the right word) by the Watergate scandal or conditions in Hitler's Germany, or that the South African morality laws prohibit mixed marriages. All that can count as critically relevant are qualities which a work may share with phenomena an understanding of which does not involve an understanding of human intentions, expectations, cultural practices, and so on.

As Wollheim insists, however, 'aesthetic object' theories of art cannot but distort critical procedure. For, typically, art criticism relates a work's second-order qualities to its first-order features – it seeks, as he puts it, to match, or to contrast, a physical property or set of properties with, say, the heightened drama or representational effects of a work (*Art and Its Objects*, pp. 178–180). Moreover if we cannot correctly identify an artwork in terms of the category to which it belongs, Kendall Walton argues in his paper, 'Categories of art', we may actually be *wrong* to ascribe certain aesthetic qualities to it. For which qualities we are able to perceive is to some extent dependent on which category (or, in some cases, categories) we see it as belonging to – e.g. classical sonata, Gothic architecture.

Nevertheless, as Walton is aware, there are no very precise procedures for determining in which categories a work is correctly perceived. As Lyas points out, we need a more thorough account of the way in which artworks are categorised and why we have the categories we do.[2] Further, to claim that in order to enjoy a work's aesthetic qualities we need to know that the object in question *is* an artwork is not to say that we cannot appreciate aesthetically whatever is before us, even if we lack knowledge of what exactly it is. It would thus be possible to respond aesthetically to, say, a Kabuki dance without knowing that it *was* a dance as distinct from, for example, a religious or social ceremony of some kind; and, similarly, with many other objects and perform-ances outside our own culture about which we might have very little knowledge. For if we took keen delight in the beauty of the gestures, the melodies or rhythmic structure of the accompaniment, the brilliance of the costumes, masks, and such like – or, alternatively, were repelled by the gro-

---

[1] The term 'aesthetic object' can, of course, be used to refer to the (physical) object regarded from an aesthetic standpoint, and therefore without commitment to theories of the kind discussed here.

[2] Review of *Contemporary Aesthetics in Scandinavia*.

tesque or jarring qualities of the movements, sounds, etc. – our interest could hardly be said to be *other* than aesthetic. No doubt we should be missing a great deal – including, perhaps, further aesthetic qualities. But, as suggested earlier, neither aesthetic nor art appreciation is an all-or-nothing achievement; like other modes of awareness, they may vary in extent and complexity.

While, therefore, considerable information and education may be necessary for the understanding of much art, and sometimes for the aesthetic appreciation of things outside art, there seem to be other cases which involve a more 'primitive' kind of aesthetic response. Nevertheless such a response represents one end of a continuum which, at its other extreme, is marked by discriminating reflection and acute critical judgment. This point will be taken up again in later chapters.

Meanwhile, in the light of the foregoing discussion, it is of interest to note Sibley's suggestion (in Part II of 'Aesthetic concepts') that there would seem to be certain interests and inclinations among people which might be encouraged in order to develop aesthetic sensitivity, and in connection with which it may be that we first learn to use words aesthetically: noticing phenomena which to begin with seize our attention because they are outstanding or unusual in some way, perhaps moving us to surprise and fear, rather than delight or distaste;[1] striking and colourful objects such as spectacular sunsets or woods in autumn; things of great size or mass, such as mountains or cathedrals, but also extremely tiny things; objects of exceptional precision and remarkable feats of skill; that which is perfectly adapted to function or ease of handling; and, by no means least, human faces, figures, and effortless movement. Without having to subscribe to Sibley's overall thesis about aesthetic concepts, we may indeed gain much from the sketch he gives here, together with that in 'Aesthetic and non-aesthetic', of how the critic (or, we might say, any aesthetic guide) typically goes about the task of trying to help people to become more observant and aesthetically aware.

It might further be suggested that not all aesthetic qualities (to continue to use the term as a convenient shorthand), call for equally acute and knowledgeable discrimination; or, to put the point differently, that some terms and expressions tend to be understood and used aesthetically more readily than others. This might depend to some extent on the sorts of objects, activities, etc. in question: some, perhaps by virtue of their physical structure or the role they play in our lives generally, may have the potential to evoke – even if they do not always sustain – an aesthetic interest, whereas others may have less.

Before concluding this chapter we may note briefly certain remarks made in connection with the dance by, first, Susanne Langer, and secondly, Mary

[1] Cf. Beardsmore, R., 'Two trends in contemporary aesthetics', pp. 364–365.

Wigman, which relate (though perhaps not obviously) to the foregoing discussion. For both deny the physicality of art in a way that does less than justice to the complexity of the concept, as well as flying in the face of established critical practice.

Although Langer rarely speaks in terms of the aesthetic, her conception of an artwork as a 'virtual entity', a 'semblance' or 'apparition' is not unlike that of Beardsley (and others) who identify the work with the aesthetic object, so separating this sharply from the physical object. Thus in her essay 'The dynamic image' Langer makes the extraordinary claim that 'In watching a dance you do not see what is physically before you – people running around or twisting their bodies; what you see is a display of interacting forces . . . .'; and again, '. . . what we really see is a virtual entity'. In the dance, she says, the physical details disappear: 'the more perfect the dance, the less we see its actualities' (*Problems of Art*, pp. 5 and 6).

Now the point Langer is after here is perfectly sound; for although she is addressing herself to the question, 'What is a dance?', rather than to the one that has been occupying us in this chapter, 'What are aesthetic qualities?', a similar logical distinction is involved. Unfortunately, however, Langer's formulation is such that what she says seems to herald a phenomenological rather than a logical account – which is (*pace* Reid[1]) precisely what is needed here. To say, 'In watching a dance . . .' and 'What we really see . . .', etc. is apt to sound as if what will come next will be a description of the spectator's actual experience in looking at a work. Hence the initial shock for the reader of being told that he does not see anything of a physical nature at all – and that, if he does, this counts against the merits of the particular dance in question.

There may indeed be some truth in the suggestion that a stress on athleticism in a dance, either in the choreography or in the performance, can make for difficulties in aesthetic appreciation – as also can a poor performance that unintentionally draws attention to the physical aspect of dance: interest may shift from the work to its manner of execution. But this is a purely contingent matter (and, to repeat, is not what Langer is concerned with). So too is the question of how far any individual, whether as a general rule or on a particular occasion, notices or fails to notice the various physical details of a dance. Langer then, in seeking to establish that an artwork *as* an artwork cannot be regarded as a purely physical phenomenon – rather as a person, *qua* person, cannot be regarded simply as a physical substance[2] – is overstating her case. Like

---

[1] Cf. *Meaning in the Arts*, pp. 83–84. (Reid's remarks here on logic as *opposed* to aesthetics are somewhat puzzling.)

[2] Comparisons between the concepts *work of art* and *person* are often drawn by philosophers. See, for example, in connection with the discussion here, Sclafani, R. J., 'The logical primitiveness of the concept of a work of art'.

Wigman's denials on the subject of dance space, Langer's too get in the way of a genuine philosophical insight.

Wigman, of course, speaks as a dancer, and some of her writings are an inspiring testimony of one who, from most accounts, was a great artist – perhaps *the* greatest within the Central European tradition of modern dance. However, in company with many another in moments of abstract reflection, she is apt to stray onto philosophical territory without recognising it. For example, she is (in effect) so concerned to make the point that our interest in the space of the dancer is different from that we normally take in the space around ourselves (or others) that she tries to insist that the dancer's realm is not physical space at all: 'it is not the tangible, limited, and limiting space of concrete reality', she says, 'but the imaginary, irrational space of the danced dimension. . . .' (*The Language of Dance*, p. 12.) We can no doubt understand what Wigman is driving at here, and *make* sense of her words, since she goes on to claim that the dancer's space 'can erase the boundaries of all corporeality . . . and turn the gesture, flowing as it is, into an image of seeming endlessness' – a poetic statement which, as such, has considerable power and aptness. But, in addition to the fact that space is never tangible anyway, there is nothing about dance space that is either irrational or imaginary (i.e., totally unrelated to physical reality); and to deny that it is physical is quite mistaken. (There may, however, be errors here in translation.)

Certainly the dance *image* – a key concept in this connection, as we shall see in the next chapter – is not in itself physical any more than is a shadow or a television screen image. Nevertheless all these *depend* on physical substances, and no satisfactory account of images in the dance can be given without reference to the tangible body of the dancer which exists in the space of 'concrete reality'. To reiterate the philosophical point here at issue: dance space (like picture space) is physical space attended to under a particular description. The differences that both Wigman and Langer are anxious to point to can therefore be elucidated without any insistence on the total 'otherness' of dance space and movement: they are differences brought about by the actively experiencing individual, with his capacity to change *at will* that perspective from which he normally views the world.

To sum up: It will be evident that, far from constituting a relatively self-contained area in the philosophy of art and aesthetics, such as the problem of metaphor and truth in literature or of symbolism in art, the question of whether there are distinctively aesthetic qualities or concepts is central to the whole enterprise of trying to define the boundaries of the aesthetic category itself. Not surprisingly, therefore, it continues to occupy, albeit in various guises, the forefront of contemporary aesthetic debate. But clarification is now sought not so much by attempting to characterise the aesthetic in terms of some state of mind without any reference to public behaviour, but rather by turning to the nature of the remarks we make about things when we attend to them in a way different from the normal mode – remarks that require a kind of justification unlike either logical deduction or empirical verification.

In traditional inquiry, however, speculations about a special mental faculty or experience have usually gone hand in hand with speculations about the nature of the aesthetic object, which, in turn, have typically centred on the beautiful. This old intuition that both these aspects, the subjective *and* the objective, have jointly to be taken into account, seems to me to have been basically sound, though needing more sophisticated philosophical treatment. 'What are aesthetic qualities?' might, indeed, be regarded as the other side of a coin on which we find 'What is the character of aesthetic experience?'; and one side cannot be considered independently of the other, though of course it is possible to give one the greater emphasis.

As we have seen, theories of aesthetic perception – cognitivist or objectivist theories,– tend to overlook, or at least to play down, the nature and importance of the response of the experiencing individual. It is this then on which we must now focus; for reference to the subjective dimension of aesthetic remarks and other manifestations of aesthetic involvement is essential, I shall maintain, to an understanding of the aesthetic mode of awareness. And this, as we shall further see, is inseparable from a consideration of the way in which aesthetic appraisals are to be justified.

CHAPTER SEVEN

Aesthetic experience

'What', it will be questioned, 'when the sun rises, do you not see a round disc somewhat like a guinea?'. 'O no, no, I see an innumerable company of the heavenly host crying, "Holy, Holy, Holy is the Lord God Almighty!"'.

William Blake: *The Vision of Judgment*

The idea that a correct account of aesthetic awareness not only allows for, but essentially demands, reference to the felt response of the experiencing subject is one that has persisted, though not unchallenged, throughout the history of aesthetic enquiry. Indeed Kant's *Critique of Judgment*, widely regarded as the foundation stone of modern philosophical aesthetics, and probably the most influential single work to be written in the subject, was designed to fill what Kant saw as a gap left by his earlier *Critique of Pure Reason* and *Critique of Practical Reason*, namely, an account of a mode of awareness to do with feeling.[1]

Moreover the response in question has long been thought of as having some kind of connection with feelings of pleasure or displeasure, delight or disgust, or (to use terms more fashionable in this context in the eighteenth century), agreeableness or disagreeableness. Thus the Analytic of the Beautiful, that part of the *Critique of Judgment* which deals with 'judgments of taste' (for which, as already suggested, we may substitute 'aesthetic appraisals'), opens with the assertion that such judgments concern the experiencing subject and his 'feeling of pleasure and pain'; while in more recent times Strawson's paper 'Aesthetic appraisal and works of art' begins with the statement:

> Many of the kinds of assessment we make are such that there is no particular relation between favourable assessment of a thing and *enjoyment* of that thing. But for some ways of praising there is a very close, though not an invariable, connection between assessing something favourably and enjoying it. This is the case with what we call aesthetic appraisal and aesthetic enjoyments.

We may note at once that Strawson does not make pleasure a necessary condition of aesthetic appreciation, but speaks only of 'a very close, though not an invariable connection' between the two (and like most philosophers focuses on

---

[1] For one of the more easily readable, but admirable, texts in the difficult field of Kantian scholarship, see Crawford, D. W., *Kant's Aesthetic Theory*.

the positive, rather than the negative aspect: on pleasure, not displeasure). Nevertheless, as Scruton suggests, whereas there is nothing unusual about saying, for instance, 'It is good to do X, but I do not like doing X', or 'X is a good man, but I take no pleasure in his company', it would be odd (logically odd) to make comparable remarks in the case of an aesthetic appraisal (*Art and Imagination*, p. 136). In other words such appraisal differs from the moral kind in (among others) this particular, having a connection with pleasure. Only in exceptional circumstances then would it make sense to say, 'It's a lovely dance, but I never enjoy watching it', or 'She dances beautifully, but I take no pleasure in seeing her move'.

However there are some who, in their attempts to argue for the objectivity of aesthetic appreciation and against any suggestion that it is all a matter of personal feeling, go to the extreme of claiming that it is not self-contradictory to say, for example, 'I admit that Raphael is a great painter, but I do not like his work; it does not move me'.[1] Similarly, G. F. Curl claims that

Many a critic has been known to make a most sensitive appraisal of a work of art in which he has made careful and subtle distinctions with great feeling and having extolled qualities of form, texture, balance and harmony, has, in spite of all these declared: 'But it's not my cup of tea',

adding that this is 'the highest form of objectivity' ('Aesthetic judgments in dance', p. 22). In both these cases this is to suppose that someone can bring a discriminating intelligence to bear on, say, a work of art, but produce a judgment that is isolated from his affective sensibilities, that reason here can be divorced from feeling. Once again aesthetic qualities are conceived of as somehow 'there' in the environment, to be *recognised* along with first-order properties independently of the perceiver's experiential response.

Yet if the connection between pleasure (or displeasure) and aesthetic awareness were only contingent, whatever enjoyment or distaste we might feel in looking at or performing a dance, listening to or playing a piece of music, etc., would be *additional* to the work in question, independent of a concern with that particular thing: it would be an effect obtainable in some other way. But in that case how is it that changes of feeling occur as we come to see a dance differently – perhaps, say, as a result of having certain features of its structure pointed out to us, or realising the significance of certain allusions or symbols it contains (e.g. the *mudras* – highly-stylised hand gestures – of some Hindu dancing)? How is it that our enjoyment of a work may be affected by further knowledge and experience of that work, or of other works, or of life more generally?

Clearly there is a different sort of connection here, on the one hand between

[1] Macdonald, M., 'Some distinctive features of arguments used in criticism of the arts', p. 121.

something regarded aesthetically and the resulting pleasure one may feel, and on the other between, for instance, a cool drink after a training session and the pleasure of slaking one's thirst. For in the second case the pleasure lies not in the drink itself (though there might be a personal preference for, say, lemonade rather than orange juice), but in the gratification of an antecedent desire or need: almost any drinkable liquid would do. Similarly with pleasant or unpleasant bodily or movement sensations: one does not, for example, find that the experience of a hot shower or inclining the body into a diagonal direction can be made more *intelligible* or can be *modified* as a result of coming to hold different *beliefs*; whereas if one is dissatisfied, say, with the ending of a dance, it is possible to trace the dissatisfied feeling to one's perception of the piece as, for instance, unresolved or, conversely, overworked rather than as concisely rounded off.

Instead of an *explanation* then of such a response, what we have here is more in the nature of a description of what the individual is responding to – the object as *constituted* by a particular sort of regard. In contrast to the pleasure or displeasure one cannot help but feel, as in the case of images produced by drugs or the sensation of dropping from a height, whatever feeling or emotion one has in the aesthetic situation results from actively 'constructing' or 'structuring' something in a certain way: 'intending' it, we might say. Attempting to characterise aesthetic appreciation by reference to the state of mind of the person so engaged, therefore, requires an elucidation of the *intentional* object (cf. p. 49 above), from which the feeling in question is inseparable. Far from endeavouring to conduct the enquiry by resorting to introspection, we have to focus on the manner in which the (physical) object is apprehended – on the character of what the individual experiences it *as* (what Kant may have meant by the *estimate* of the form of an object: see Schaper's 'The pleasures of taste').

This brings us then to a consideration of that cluster of concepts mentioned in Chapter 5, which includes *disinterested contemplation, imagination, form*, and the idea of taking an interest in something *for its own sake*. None of these is easy to deal with separately in relation to aesthetic appreciation, since each tends to overlap with the others. But, for reasons that may become evident as we proceed, I shall begin with the notion of disinterested contemplation, which, if only by virtue of the term itself, is liable to give rise to a good deal of misunderstanding and perplexity. For one thing, a common use of 'contemplation', drawing on the etymological connection with 'temple', carries the meaning of 'meditation on spiritual things'; and even if the association with the idea of 'the contemplative life' or being 'a contemplative' does not suggest a similarity between aesthetic and religious (or *quasi*-religious) experience, there is still some danger that the term may imply an absence of concern with a particular object available to sense perception.

Again, while it seems natural to speak of contemplating, say, a piece of sculpture, a mountain, or other things that are – to all appearances, at any rate – static and unchanging, 'contemplation' would not seem to be a word that is ordinarily used in the case of that which is transient or unfolds in time, such as a dance or a piece of music. Such a term might be in order, it might be thought, in respect of the visitor to an art gallery or the nature lover leaning on a gate admiring the view; but how can it apply to an audience that can hardly keep still, so infectious are the rhythms and moods of a dance or a musical work (let alone to the performers themselves)?

As regards the first point – the idea of meditating on some kind of 'higher reality' – the importance cannot be emphasised too strongly of the fact that in aesthetic contemplation there is always some object either immediately present to the senses or, as in the case of literature, accessible to experience through perceptual means. Unless, for example, a dancer is there to be seen, he cannot be seen *as* graceful or grotesque; unless there are sounds available to hearing, music cannot be heard *as* soothing or plaintive. Attention is thus directed outwards to something in the external world that is publicly recognisable.

Secondly, as well as avoiding the mistake of identifying stillness with inactivity, we should be aware that 'contemplation' as used in aesthetic theory, especially in conjunction with 'disinterested', has become more or less a technical term. We thus find it extended to listening as well as to looking, and to the activity of creative and performing artists as well as to their audiences. Reid, for instance, observes:

A dancer or actor in the full activity of dancing or acting is often, perhaps always, in some degree contemplating the product of his own activity. In playing a musical instrument it is very important to *listen* to one's own playing ('Movement and meaning', p. 9).

And Michael Oakeshott:

Painting a picture, composing a verbal image, making a tune, are themselves the activities of contemplation which constitute poetic imagining ('The voice of poetry in the conversation of mankind', p. 232).

It would, indeed, be a mistake to deny an aesthetic concern to the creative artist – except, of course, in the case of those individuals who, as we saw in Chapter 5, set out specifically to produce *anti*-aesthetic pieces. For artists compose not in a vacuum, but against the background of certain assumptions about what is likely to happen to their work when it is completed – how, so to speak, it will be received; in other words, against the background of what they believe to be the attitudes and expectations of those to whom their work is 'addressed' (though it is artists themselves who are mainly responsible for shaping and changing those attitudes and expectations). It would also be quite erroneous to suppose that there are two separate sorts of activity going on during the creating of a work – on the one hand, some observable performance such as stepping and gesturing, writing, drawing, etc., and, on the other, some putative inner process of contemplating, judging, reflecting on what is evolving, and feeling satisfied or dissatisfied as the case may be. Rather, the artist's appraisal is expressed *in* his activity. 'That's a weak transition', 'Too many developments are taking place at once here', and such like, are not necessarily said aloud, but are manifested in the deletions, the additions and alterations that he makes (Cf. Charlton: 'Aestheticism', p. 127).

Dancers, actors, singers, instrumentalists, and – most notably, perhaps – conductors also demonstrate their appreciation, their understanding of a work, *in* their performances: their interpretations *are* their appraisals (though the issue here is altogether more complex inasmuch as direction by someone else may be involved, and in any performance by more than one person, each might have only a partial grasp of the work as a whole).

When Strawson speaks of aesthetic enjoyments taking their place among spectator enjoyments[1] then, this would seem to mean, not (as Charlton appears to think) that aesthetic pleasure is restricted to the spectator as against, say, the dancer or the engraver, but that the idea of spectator enjoyments is *logically prior* to the idea of participant enjoyments. That is, in order to understand the notion of aesthetic interest we have to understand what it is to be interested in something as it exists for being looked at or listened to – for contemplation. And as Wollheim points out in the context of another discussion, while not all spectators are artists, all artists – including, it might be added, performing artists – are spectators (*Arts and Its Objects*, p. 108).

Equally liable to misinterpretation is the term 'disinterested'. Quite apart from the growing use of the word nowadays to mean *un*interested, which of course is not what it signifies in the aesthetic context, a potential difficulty is that this is another term which has a *quasi*-technical use in aesthetics. But it is doubtful, as Stolnitz suggests, whether we can understand modern aesthetic theory unless we understand the concept of disinterestedness; it is a 'major watershed' in the history of the subject ('On the origins of "aesthetic disinterestedness"', p. 131 and p. 139). For, originating in the eighteenth century as an ethical concept standing in opposition to that of self-interest, but later extended to the perception of beautiful things, it was largely responsible for aesthetic awareness coming to be understood as of a distinctive kind. At the same time, as we have already seen, it made way for the revolutionary view of

---

[1] 'Aesthetic appraisal and works of art', p. 180.

art as autonomous – something to be valued over and above any usefulness it might have, i.e. on *sui generis* grounds.

Nevertheless, as an aesthetic concept, disinterestedness is related to its ethical predecessor inasmuch as the concern of the aesthetically engaged individual is with what is outside himself, outside that which, in a discussion of perfection, goodness and reality as related both to conduct and to art, Iris Murdoch calls 'the fat relentless ego'. Great art, she says, can teach us how things 'can be looked at and loved without being seized and used, without being appropriated into the greedy organism of the self'.[1] This captures that feature of disinterested contemplation which involves the contrast of aesthetic interest not only with desires and appetites of the sensuous kind, but also with practical and theoretical concerns. The object is not used or manipulated for the achievement of an end, neither is it a focus of interest having to do with explanation and information about, for example, its causes and consequences, how it works or is made.

As regards the contrast with *practical* concerns, aesthetic experience does not involve engaging in or attending to something with a further aim in mind – though it is possible, of course, at the same time to appreciate a dance, an anthem, an ode, etc. as serving some function (we may recall Urmson's point that interest in something may be multiply-grounded: cf. p.47 above). This ruling out of means-ends considerations in aesthetic appreciation is connected with the crucially important idea of the *uniqueness* of whatever is regarded aesthetically. For a particular end or aim, like the satisfaction of a need or desire, might be achieved by a variety of means. Physical fitness, for instance, could be promoted by this dance as well as that – or by some other activity altogether, such as swimming; release from emotional strain might be effected by various dances, not just *this* one – or, again, by drugs, say, or psychotherapy.

The contrasting of aesthetic awareness with *theoretical* interest involves a set of rather more complex issues. In the first place, the notion of disinterestedness rules out a concern with propositional knowledge: as I tried to show in the previous chapter, aesthetic appreciation *presupposes* factual discourse but is not itself a species of it, and whatever empirically verifiable properties the object or activity has do not feature in the aesthetic appraisal itself. To repeat what has been said earlier: such an appraisal may be reasonable or unreasonable, fitting or unfitting, but it does not involve a claim to truth or falsity (though this is not to deny, as I shall discuss in a moment, that aesthetic awareness may deepen or even bring about fresh understanding of what we already know).

Secondly, the non-theoretical character of aesthetic interest involves the distinction between an object understood in terms of its being, say, a ballet, a tree or a jewel – i.e. a member of a class – and the object experienced

---

[1] *The Sovereignty of Good*, p. 59ff; cf. also p. 85ff.

aesthetically, precisely *not* as a member of a class or instance of a kind. It is not then identifiable in terms of a set of characteristics common to each and every member of a class or kind; its qualities or features cannot be stated in advance. Once more the uniqueness criterion is highlighted – though again it does not follow that at the same time that we apprehend something aesthetically we may not also recognise it as, for example, a dance rather than a play or an athletic contest; or, further, as belonging to a particular sub-category such as a gavotte, a tango, or a three-act ballet. To claim that aesthetic appreciation is non-theoretical in the sense of being non-conceptual is to say that the object cannot be *classified* as, say, graceful or hideous or well-proportioned: there are no universal principles to which all graceful or hideous or well-proportioned objects must conform in the way that it is, and must be, possible for there to be criteria for identifying something as a dance or, further, as a gavotte, a tango, and so on.

To make the point another way. If such general principles *were* available, appreciation could proceed by rule of thumb. Whether the thing was beautiful, for instance, could be 'read off' mechanically, the relevant features being checked against a list of requirements so that the conclusion could be reached: 'Yes, this is beautiful', 'No, that is not'. Such a suggestion rightly strikes us as absurd; for our response to beauty – and other aesthetic qualities – is direct, unmediated: we do not *think* about other properties and then *infer* from them that the object is or is not a beautiful (or witty, profound, amusing, etc.) object.

If, indeed, specifications could be mapped out blueprint fashion, anyone could in principle become a brilliant sculptor, playwright, choreographer, and so on; for there could be master-plans, recipes, formulae, guaranteed to ensure success. A choreographer, for example, might have to aim at a wealth of inventiveness; depth of feeling and human interest; plenty of contrast and variety; dramatic power; intricacy and complexity; and so forth. Yet it is obvious that although any of these features might be precisely what contributes to the success of a particular dance, there could be other works, equally success-ful, that do *not* share such features. Their merit might in fact lie in quite con-trasting attributes – in their simplicity, say, rather than their complexity; their comic, rather than their dramatic power; their cool beauty rather than a concern with human situations and events. Not only that, but a dance might fail, or at any rate have deficiencies, precisely in virtue of what, in another work, makes for excellence. Further, if there *were* fixed criteria, specifiable in advance, looking at and listening to works of art would be a once-and-for all experience. We should be unlikely to find it rewarding, as we certainly do with many works, to return to them over and over again, constantly discovering new surprises and delights.

The question 'What makes a good – or beautiful or profound or funny – dance?', etc. has, therefore, to be distinguished from the radically different question 'What makes *this* – say, Frederick Ashton's *Symphonic Variations* – a beautiful dance?' Unlike the first, this question does not ask about good or beautiful dances *in general,* but about one particular work that is already available for contemplation. It arises, and can properly arise, only *after* something has been experienced: aesthetic appraisal, as Meager has convincingly argued in her paper 'The uniqueness of a work of art', is *a posteriori,* involving each case being taken on its merits. There is thus always a concrete point of reference, with observable features that can be picked out to back up (or perhaps overthrow) whatever claim is made.

This feature of *uniqueness* as a criterion of aesthetic interest also underlines what Wollheim calls the Acquaintance principle (*Art and Its Objects,* p. 233); that is, aesthetic judgments (unlike moral judgments, for instance), have to be based on a direct encounter with whatever is in question. The qualities of a particular object have to be experienced at first hand in precisely that conjunction which makes it what it is *as* an aesthetic object: they are not discriminable independently of the object. Rather as a person is not a specimen of a class of, say, interesting or lovable persons, even if he or she *is* interesting or lovable (and even though he or she is a member of the class of humans), so a dance cannot be catalogued as a specimen of, for example, *beautiful* dances. In neither case is there a general kind, with a prescribed or prescribable set of properties: each individual of whom the claim is made is uniquely interesting or lovable or beautiful (and so on) just in virtue of the particular combination of attributes we see manifested in that individual. Consequently an object of aesthetic enjoyment is, like a person, wholly irreplaceable, whatever the resemblances to another there might be or whatever similar functions each might serve. As Wittgenstein puts it:

> You *could* select either of two poems to remind you of death, say. But supposing you had read a poem and admired it, could you say: 'Oh, read the other, it will do the same?'. . .
> If I admire a minuet I can't say, 'Take another. It does the same thing'. What do you mean? It *is* not the same (*Lectures and Conversations on Aesthetics,* IV, p. 34).

So far, however, and perhaps not surprisingly in view of the negative overtones of the term *dis*interestedness, the character of aesthetic experience has been sketched chiefly in terms of what is *not* involved. But before we consider a more positive aspect, it may be as well in view of what has been said above to stress again that, while *logically* distinct, an aesthetic concern may, *experientially* speaking, exist in conjunction with other concerns: it may be (and often is) part of a larger, more complex whole, a single thread, as it were, in a many-stranded texture. Thus, although most human beings are obliged to spend a good deal of their time carrying out practical and theoretical pursuits, this does not mean that during those pursuits, or possibly interspersed with them, there may not be moments, or perhaps longer periods, when attention takes on an aesthetic dimension. For example, a notator engaged in recording a dance might be aesthetically moved from time to time by the sheer beauty of the movement.

Aesthetic interest may even take over from other sorts of interest. Becoming caught up with, say, a speaker's attractive appearance, the elegance of his gestures, his style of delivery, and so forth, we may lose touch with *what* he is saying and pay more attention to the overall presentation: to movement, colour, sound, etc., for itself, for its own sake. This leads to an important question to which we shall return later about the significance – or otherwise – of the context in which an object of aesthetic awareness is set. At this point, however, we need to address ourselves to the question of what, more precisely, can be meant by attending to something *for its own sake*.

This rather curious expression (which David Pole is perhaps right in thinking is apt to be used rather glibly in aesthetics[1]), is not readily amenable to alternative formulation. It also to some extent takes us back over ground already visited. For one thing, it draws attention yet again to the disinterested character of aesthetic awareness; for whereas to be involved in something for the sake of money, say, or for the sake of one's family[2] indicates some further concern, specifiable apart from the 'something', for *its* own sake suggests an overriding interest in the 'thing' itself.

This points up the problem of how the 'it' within 'itself' is to be characterised. But if we now bear in mind the non-conceptual feature of aesthetic appraisal discussed a moment ago, it would seem that, in *not* viewing something as a member of a class we regard it as belonging to a realm in some way different from that of everyday reality. The intentional object is, in a word – though a word that can all too easily be misunderstood in this context – an *illusion*, a product of that capacity we have to imagine things, events, situations, activities and states of affairs as different from how we know them in fact to be. The object we 'posit' (to borrow a useful term of Scruton's[3]) is, we might say, an object of the external world seen *as if* it made present, vivid to perception, what we know to be absent. To speak of attending to something for its own sake is thus bound up with the idea of *imagination*.

We have, yet again, to be careful here. For such talk might suggest delusion or self-deception; unreal, imaginary 'objects' of a kind like Macbeth's dagger; an unearthly world 'behind' the ordinary space-time world; and so on. But

[1] 'Art, imagination and Mr. Scruton', p. 199.

[2] Cf. Charlton, W., 'Aestheticism', p. 127; see also the discussion of 'for its own sake' in his *Aesthetics*.

[3] *The Aesthetics of Architecture*, ch. 4 (a very useful chapter for all these concepts at present under discussion).

imagination is a concept of considerable intricacy, applicable to a variety of states of mind that range from a highly active to a purely passive kind; and the sort of mental activity in which we engage in the aesthetic situation is quite different from, for example, hallucinations or other products of a *suffering* mind. Far from involving a total loss of awareness of ordinary reality, aesthetic experience is rooted in an awareness of that reality; but, by an act of will, by freely choosing, we are able to construe it differently, knowing full well what we are doing and having no difficulty in recognising the difference, however, powerful the 'illusion'. We keep, so to speak, the two modes of awareness apart – which is precisely why we are able to *relate* one to the other, not, as in cases of *de*lusion, confounding them.

Another way of making the point that imaginative activity presupposes a grasp of commonplace reality – which, in this context, is also to reassert the logical dependence of aesthetic perception on ordinary perception – is to say that to attend to something for its own sake, in its own right, requires an understanding of things as *not* in their own right, but as fitting into some scheme in a world where dealing with practical and theoretical tasks predominates. In aesthetic experience we enjoy the appearance of 'purposiveness without purpose', in Kant's arresting phrase; or as C. J. Ducasse puts it:

> Slang paraphrases the assertion that an object is beautiful by saying that it is 'easy to look at'. . . . To be 'easy to look at' is to be *as if made for the purpose* . . . (*The Philosophy of Art*, p. 239).

Such imagining then is not, for instance, that species of imaginative conjecturing which E. J. Furlong, in his book *Imagination*, distinguishes as a kind of 'supposing' (one that often plays an important part in theoretical disciplines such as history, science and philosophy). Nor has it to do with imaginary phenomena such as dreams or after-images; we are not, in aesthetic experience, having mental images over which we can exert no control.[1] As members of a theatre or television audience, spectators in an art gallery, readers of novels, and so forth, we are not victims of deceptions, counterfeits or lies. Neither are dancers or actors, for instance, concerned with perpetrating such frauds, as Plato seems to have thought (so leading him to exclude from his ideal state poets, dramatists and painters – though not, it may be noted, musicians or architects). Hence, significantly, we speak in such cases of *make*-believe: the 'Let's pretend' element is clearly understood on both sides of the 'curtain'.

Both logically and psychologically there is thus a fundamental connection, and yet at the same time a fundamental distinction, between reality and

---

[1] For further discussion of various aspects of the concept of imagination with particular reference to the dance, see my essay on the subject in *Concepts in Modern Educational Dance*.

imaginative illusion. Logically, aesthetic interest presupposes that everyday interest in gestures, words, objects, etc. which centres on the uses to which they may be put, but it constitutes a distinct mode of experiencing them. Psychologically, we always retain at least a minimal awareness of what is actually the case, even though we may become so caught up in the experience as almost to forget the world of ordinary reality.

To speak in terms of 'illusion' and 'as if', however, as part of an account of aesthetic interest, must not be taken as suggesting that in actual experience we think by analogy, seeing something *as if it were*, say, graceful, austere, unified. That is, in attending to something aesthetically we do not *think* of it in a certain way *in addition to watching* it, nor do we make comparisons or analogies and then bring to bear on our perceptions some particular interpretation: we simply see it *as* graceful, unified, etc.

This capacity that the human being has to shift his perspective from the workaday scene to an imaginative realm in which things are, as it were, self-contained unities, would seem to be related in some way to his capacity for play. Indeed in his thought-provoking book *Homo Ludens*, the eminent Dutch historian, Johannes Huizinga, traces an etymological link between the words 'play' and 'illusion'. The latter, he suggests, is 'a pregnant word which means literally "in-play" (from *inlusion, illudere*, or *inludere*)'; and both play and aesthetic activity derive, he argues, from 'the impulse to create orderly form'.

The notion of *form* as a criterion of aesthetic awareness, however, is another that has to be treated with care. For if we were to understand it as implying that all objects of aesthetic interest exhibit harmony, balance, or other such formal qualities, we should be back with the idea of antecedently specifiable characteristics of a general kind, thus denying the uniqueness condition and reducing aesthetic appraisals to observations of the empirical variety. The term 'form' is, moreover, notoriously ambiguous both outside and within aesthetic discourse, where it is sometimes used simply in place of 'shape'; sometimes to denote specific compositional structures such as canon or theme and variations; sometimes by way of contrast either with subject matter or with content; and sometimes in a quite general way to do with any ordered sequence or arrangement of elements.

From consideration of this last sense it is clear that form is not a sufficient condition of aesthetic interest; for we often appreciate how well something is structured *without* regarding it aesthetically. For instance, admiration of the manner in which the various episodes of a well-executed javelin throw fit together, so achieving a certain flow and smooth efficiency, might consist simply in an appreciation of how everything is appropriately organised for the fulfilment of a particular purpose. Such cases are typically those for which there can be copybook models, blueprints for action. There is a clear-cut ideal which all serious endeavour strives to match; and pleasure in the attainment of the goal in an economical way might derive precisely from that. But although such pleasure can co-exist with aesthetic pleasure, the two are not the same. On the contrary, the satisfaction we find in whatever is regarded aesthetically involves our perceiving its ingredients as *seeming* to work together *as if* for some purpose, even if it may not have – and may not be intended to have – any practical outcome: we enjoy a purposive *quality* of what we see or hear, independently of any knowledge or understanding of the actual or possible uses of the object or activity we contemplate. Kant's idea of 'the mere form of purposiveness' is a way of drawing attention, Schaper says, 'to configurations that appear to be patterned . . . without our being able to say what the pattern is *for*, except that it seems to be for our enjoyment'; we approach things aesthetically 'when, despite being unable to say *that* they exhibit purpose, we approach them *as if* they did' (*Studies in Kant's Aesthetics*, p. 125).

To see something as having form, then, is a logical requirement of aesthetic experience. It is to. see the object as marked off, so to speak, from its ordinary surroundings, discontinuous with everyday things and events, 'out of' the normal space and time we inhabit. The concept of form is, indeed, vital to understanding how it is that we can talk of aesthetic enjoyment in cases where the idea of enjoyment might at first glance seem totally out of place – works of art, say, having to do with grief, suffering or death. For how, we may ask, could it be supposed that anyone – except some thoroughly depraved individual – could take delight in contemplating the distress of others or the folly and weakness of human beings that lead to their downfall and destruction? R. A. Sharpe, for example, writes:

> We would feel that it demonstrates a failure to respond to *King Lear* if we were to claim that we enjoyed it. The work is too great and too tragic. It might impress, overwhelm or stun us; but 'mere' enjoyment would suggest that the audience responded merely to its narrative merits ('Hearing-as', p. 217).

But a representational work is not a tale dressed up, as it were, in words, movement, and so forth, something separable from the particular medium. What we contemplate in the arts when we attend to them aesthetically are not (for example) the calamities and misfortunes that actually befall our fellow creatures, not raw emotions actually suffered and lived through, but the *presentation* of such disasters and emotions. In other words it is the structured form in which they *appear* – what Aristotle termed *mythos*[1] – that is the object of our

---

[1] *Poetics*, chs. 6–14. There is a wealth of exegesis and comment on this idea: see, for example, Else, G. F., *Aristotle's Poetics*, and (more briefly) Schaper, E., *Prelude to Aesthetics*, ch. 3, s.3.

admiration and delight: the events and situations that are depicted have a different character from that which they would have in real life and consequently require a different mental 'set'. To repeat, they are *make-believe, fictions*; and enjoying things aesthetically is thus not incompatible with feeling overwhelmed, outraged, appalled, and indeed a great variety of emotions.

This formal feature of the concept of aesthetic interest (a *logical* condition) has then to be distinguished from a particular (i.e. *critical*) appraisal such as that something is finely-proportioned or tightly-knit. Even if seen as diffuse or uneven or lacking balance, it nevertheless, as an object of aesthetic regard, has form in this logical sense. Or, more accurately, the percipient *gives* it form, placing boundaries around it, as it were, setting it apart from ordinary reality. On the other hand what is conspicuously well made readily lends itself to aesthetic contemplation, and it is thus hardly surprising that aesthetic interest is likely to be evoked and sustained by many works of art. For the creating of a great number of dances, poems, plays, etc. presupposes their being regarded as self-sufficient wholes, and their structuring is such as to facilitate imaginative attention and aesthetic enjoyment.

The artist working within the tradition of using a sensuous medium to create an illusion – a tradition that has dominated art practice for over two hundred years – might in fact be looked on as a sort of director who guides and controls in large measure what is perceived in a work. For an art medium is not simply the physical substance he uses:[1] it is something more than, say, bodily movement or the oils the painter mixes in his palette, but involves also (as indicated in Chapter 4) a network or system of conventions which determine how such phenomena should be approached, and what, within flexible limits, may be seen. Our appreciation of form, in the sense at present under discussion, is thus assisted both by the artist and by the institutional 'surroundings' in which those works are set. We do not, for instance, see a dancer's movements within the dance as all one with the movements he makes when he takes his curtain call largely because of that curtain and other theatre practices; neither do we take the orchestra's tuning-up sounds as part of the musical programme.

Indeed a whole battery of devices and techniques is usually employed both within artworks and in their presentation to set them off from the ordinary environment, and so to prompt and reinforce an aesthetic stance. On the one hand there are the contextual controls that are *internal* to the work itself, brought about by the technique and artistry of the composer. These range from the time-honoured opening of many stories, 'Once upon a time' and simply-organised, yet essentially artificial, rhythms and patterns of various sorts to highly-stylised language, sound, movement, etc. On the other hand there are *external* means such as darkened auditoria, lighted stages or arenas set apart, however slightly,

---

[1] Cf. Binkley, T., 'Piece: contra aesthetics'.

from those who watch and listen, which are designed to encourage a readiness to enter an illusory world, to entertain fictions. In the theatre the rising of the curtain is thus a significant (for many, a magical) moment, serving a purpose similar to 'Once upon a time'.

An important factor in this connection in the case of the dance – though one the significance of which is often overlooked here, perhaps because it is so often taken for granted – is the sound accompaniment, whether musical or otherwise. For dance time is not clock time; but whereas rhythm and phrasing impinge powerfully on the ear (as well as reverberating, so to speak, throughout the body of the dancer), they are not always so immediately or vividly apparent to the average spectator in the absence of sound. Even when there are counter- or cross-rhythms as between movement and sound, looking may be sharpened simply because of this contrast. In any case the movements we see almost continually around us in the course of daily life normally have no special connection with any sounds that may also happen to be going on.

If, however, in the aesthetic situation the object of attention is separated off from its normal context to stand apart in a kind of isolation, this does not mean that aesthetic experience is divorced from either an understanding of or a concern with the everyday world. On the contrary, especially in the case of a good deal of art, it may enlarge and intensify that understanding and concern. For there is a sense in which, in responding to something aesthetically, we may *realise* in a peculiarly vivid way what we already know, yet seem to learn for the first time. That is, our experience is such that our knowledge gains a new dimension; in Keats' striking phrase, it is 'proved on the pulses'. An anthropologist, for example, sensitive to such things as the subtly changing rhythms of a ritual dance, its floor patterns and varying group formations, might well find his theoretical understanding of a tribe's attitudes to, say, death, war, or the various seasons reinforced and sharpened. Details such as the precision and timing of movements performed in unison might *bring home* to him, as no factual description or explanation could, the power and significance of participation in communal dance of this kind.

In one sense, as Beardsmore[1] argues, the observer learns nothing new; in another he learns profoundly new truths. For the picture he now has is changed: what was previously known in a general way becomes illumined in a particular, often startling manner. The learning involved is of a kind different from the 'learning-that' variety; it is not so much that one is *told* something as *shown* 'what it is like'. This *quasi*-revelatory effect of much great art, or 'poetic shock', is much discussed in respect of literature; but there is considerable scope also, for obvious reasons, in the dance and allied art forms such as mime and dance-

---

[1] 'Two trends in contemporary aesthetics', sections 2 and 3.

mime, where details of people's behaviour previously observed only vaguely or imprecisely are often arrestingly revealed.

Hepburn, however, draws attention to this kind of 'realising' or 'coming-to-be-aware', as he calls it, in connection also with the aesthetic appreciation of nature, and further suggests that here there can be 'a reflexive effect by which the spectator experiences *himself* in an unusual and vivid way'.[1] This insight might be extended, I submit, to the case of the performing artist; for inasmuch as what is presented by a dancer, a singer or an actor is actualised through the person himself, he may feel a 'new' person. We might then adapt the passage from Barbara Hepworth's writings that Hepburn quotes appreciatively:

> what a different shape and 'being' one becomes lying on the sand with the sea almost above from when standing against the wind on a sheer high cliff with seabirds circling patterns below one . . .

and say, 'What a different shape and "being" one becomes' with, for instance, in Wigman's words:

> the feet planted powerfully against the floor, jerking up in staccato rhythm, or, under the arched span, thrusting forward like the sharp point of a dagger. . . . The arms in short, angular gestures sharply bent, or motionless, tautly stretched out. . . . Horizontal against vertical. Dimension against dimension. . . . (*The Language of Dance*, p. 56).

Such experiences which involve a fresh or added element to understanding nevertheless confirm rather than undermine the claim that aesthetic awareness is not a species or source of propositional knowledge. For they are possible precisely because of, not despite, the imaginative character of such awareness. Notwithstanding talk of art 'holding a mirror up to nature' and so forth, a faithful imitation of what is or has been would, on the contrary, be something *other* than aesthetic. Of course many representational works are *based* on historical personages or situations and events that have actually occurred; but to attempt to reproduce 'pictures' of them that were correct in every particular, whether in words, gestures, drawings, or whatever, would be to record or document rather than to create. Unlike a journalist, a historian, or a social scientist, whose job it is to seek out and report propositional truths, an artist is not tied to actualities but is free either to *re*present aspects of the real world – highlighting, intensifying, perhaps exaggerating certain details – or to explore what *might* have happened, what *might* be, now or in the future.

Our understanding of the world and of the human condition may thus be

---

[1] 'Contemporary aesthetics and the neglect of natural beauty', p. 289.

extended, even transformed, through art because we are required to reflect not so much on realities, but on possibilities; and this, not by means of imaginative hypothesising ('supposing'), as in science or history or philosophy, but by contemplating concrete images presented in a sensuous medium. A representational work then is not a copy; indeed it brings us face to face with, for example, a *unique* tragedy or comedy, a *particular* shade of joy, sorrow or fear, an *unrepeatable* piece of foolishness or heroism. Instead of describing such things in general terms, it presents a specific manifestation – and with great art, in ways that are not only credible but persuasive and compelling.

However, the freedom of the artist both to enliven and deepen understanding of what is already familiar and to open up new conceptions of what the world *might* be like, how people *might* behave, raises certain problems. For what is portrayed may seem implausible. This might, of course, be due to lack of knowledge and experience, emotional immaturity, and the like, on the part of those who watch or listen or read. To appreciate Antony Tudor's *Dark Elegies*, for instance, is partly a matter of having, so to speak, lived long enough – of having, in John Casey's felicitous phrase, 'a sufficient sense of bearings' (*The Language of Criticism*, p. 24). On the other hand there may be serious flaws in the work itself: rather than illumine, it may smudge or distort. Yet since there can be no appeal to a set of *actual* experiences, even if it is on that *sort* of experience that the artist draws, and against such a background that the public approaches his art, how is a work that is capable of extending horizons, of enlarging and refining sensibilities, to be distinguished from one that blurs and blunts? How, to speak more generally, is the plausibility of fictions (in a generous sense of the term), to be tested?

Such a vital issue merits a chapter to itself, since it involves nothing less than a consideration of how aesthetic appraisals are to be justified. Yet this is not a an issue that is separate from an account of the nature of aesthetic appreciation; for to distinguish the kind of verification procedures appropriate to a particular mode of experience is crucial for an understanding of the distinctiveness of that mode.

We still have, however, a question left over from our earlier discussion of the possibility of aesthetic interest arising, as it were, 'out of the blue'; that is, to what extent is it essential for aesthetic appreciation of something that account be taken of the context in which it is set?

Now it has become almost a commonplace of contemporary aesthetic philosophy that aesthetic appraisal of an object (like moral appraisal, for instance), does indeed require a grasp of the framework or 'environment' of the object (or action, etc.). In Wittgenstein's words, 'the surroundings give it its importance' (*Philosophical Investigations*, para. 583). This is undoubtedly true in a great many cases, and in the aesthetic realm applies especially in respect of art, though it is clear that the surroundings (in a quite straightforward sense of the word) may play a major role too as regards the aesthetic interest of, say, a tree, a lake or a building. Yet there seem to be other occasions when the context of something is ignored or unnoticed or seemingly forgotten, and aesthetic qualities 'jump' out of their immediate framework in a vivid, startling manner, having no relevance to the particular situation or circumstances – as, for example, when we are struck by the elegant appearance and style of a speaker in a dreary lecture hall, or, to take Bullough's famous example, during a fog at sea.

Perhaps what is needed, therefore, is some differentiation of types of context in the aesthetic situation. We might distinguish, for instance: 1), that sort which consists in the particular gestures, words, sounds, etc. immediately surrounding the one(s) in question; 2), the larger sort made up of, say, a whole work of art or one clearly-defined section such as the coda or the second act; 3), the particular art form or genre with its particular conventions; 4), the wider historical and/or cultural setting in which the 'utterance' or performance occurs, including – as notably in the case of the theatre – certain institutionalised practices; and 5), more broadly still, the whole 'form of life' context in which the object or activity is, so to speak, embedded, and certain attitudes and habits deeply ingrained. That is, there would seem to be contexts within contexts, smaller structures and items within larger ones – the latter usually lending themselves to a greater range of interpretation and requiring more skill for their understanding inasmuch as many differing elements need to be held together, imaginatively integrated.

The need for such distinctions is illustrated by Scruton's discussion in *Art and Imagination* (chapters 10 and 11 especially) of the notion of appreciating something for its own sake. For Scruton is aware that if, lacking knowledge of the Japanese language and of the conventions of Japanese theatre, he goes to a Noh play – perhaps even ignorant of the fact that it *is* a play – he may nevertheless enjoy what he sees and hears simply as a sequence of movements and sounds. Yet this he finds ironic, since although (quite rightly, in my view), Scruton sees the elucidation of the 'it' within 'for its own sake' as vital for any satisfactory analysis of aesthetic interest, he takes this interest to involve an understanding of what the object or activity *is* – a play, a ballet, a game, or whatever:[1] in other words, in terms of its membership of a class. He is therefore puzzled that, in the hypothetical situation he imagines, he would have to say, 'I was not treating it as a play; I took a merely aesthetic interest in what I saw' (cf. Strawson's remarks about paintings and football referred to on p. 55 above).

It might, however, be suggested that appreciation will vary according to the context or contexts of which the spectator is aware. Thus in the case of a Noh

---

[1] Cf. my remarks on a similar position adopted by Best (among others) in my 'Aesthetic qualities in the dance and their significance in education', p. 175ff.

play there is the sequence of movements and sounds that may be seen *as* a play, set moreover in the highly culture-bound context of Japanese theatre. But even if someone could not identify it as such and could not comprehend it within *that* context, he might still approach it with aesthetic expectations, taking for granted (as with Western theatre) that 'setting apart' from ordinary life of what is fictional. Another person, perhaps under the impression that the proceedings were, say, some kind of religious ritual rather than a theatre event, might also find aesthetic satisfaction in what he saw and heard. And at yet another, more rudimentary level, as in the case of a child (provided he belonged to a culture possessing the concept of the aesthetic), there might be simply that readiness to regard things aesthetically without much concern for or understanding of what the 'thing' was.

A question that now arises is how one level of appreciation might affect or interact with another. For Scruton claims that when he discovers that what he is watching is a play, his interest will change and he will attend to quite different features of what is before him – though he does not indicate what sort of features these are, or whether the 'it' that is up for identification has altered completely or has merely acquired an additional dimension. If, of course, someone lacks knowledge that is required in order to understand certain intentions of the artist, he might well *mis*-take an artwork, or at any rate respond inadequately. But while he may not appreciate the *work*, this is not to say that he is devoid of any aesthetic interest in it: to say that he does not appraise it *as a play* (for example) is to say something else. The only sort of experience that is essential for aesthetic appreciation seems to be that involving the recognition of spatial and temporal elements which make up visual and auditory structures of varying complexity. For it is possible, as Hepburn points out, to see sand-dunes and rocks (say) simply as coloured shapes, as when we look at them with our head between our legs;[1] and encountering some artworks from alien cultures, it might be added, may not be altogether unlike seeing the world upside down, or as we sometimes see things on first awaking in unfamiliar surroundings, when we cannot rightly tell what it is that we are looking at.

It would certainly be unfortunate if aesthetic experience were to be regarded as in some way extraordinary, abnormal, infrequent or esoteric, a difficult achievement reserved for special times and occasions – as may result if art is taken as the paradigm of aesthetic interest, and as also might be suggested by our resorting to expressions such as 'ordinary life', 'everyday experience', 'normal perception', etc. in order to draw attention to a contrasting mode of awareness. Sometimes, however, philosophers do speak in such a way as to make it sound as though this were the case. Stuart Hampshire, for instance (though it may be that he is simply rather careless here in his choice of terms),

[1] 'Contemporary aesthetics and the neglect of natural beauty', p. 295.

states in 'Logic and appreciation' that 'to hold attention still upon any particular thing is unnatural' (p. 166); while Schaper writes that 'seeing things aesthetically requires a special effort' (*Prelude to Aesthetics*, p. 83). Stolnitz, on the other hand, claims that 'aesthetic perception is not something rare and exotic, unless life is so lived that it comes to be considered unnatural'. 'What', he asks, 'could be more natural than simply to look out upon the world and take interest in its sights and sounds, its movements and expressiveness?' (*Aesthetics and the Philosophy of Art Criticism*, p. 44).

To speak of the activities of human beings in terms of what is 'natural' or 'unnatural', however, is fraught with difficulties. Stolnitz, it is true, is to some extent cautious here with his 'in a sense', and such like; but he nonetheless tends to gloss over the fact that a disposition to attend to things aesthetically, whether in situations designed specifically for such attention or otherwise, is learned, or at least 'picked up', from the culture to which the individual belongs no less than is that attitude which encourages enquiries of the sort, 'How does that work?', 'How did it come to be here?', etc. In other words a readiness simply to stand and stare, or to engage in rhythmic and patterned movement or sound-making for its own sake, is one of a whole complex of habits and practices that is fostered and provided for in varying ways and to varying degrees (or perhaps not at all) according to the particular culture or sub-culture. Clearly, for aesthetic sensibility to *develop*, particularly in respect of the arts, effort *is* required, as well as knowledge from other fields. Nevertheless Stolnitz is right to urge that there is nothing strange or fundamentally difficult about adopting an aesthetic stance, even if some people might live in a situation in which such a stance is not consistently nurtured or cultivated in any depth.

It would seem then that under the general heading of 'aesthetic awareness' a range of experience is possible, and that aesthetic appraisals are enormously varied. Some involve a good deal of intellectual effort and discrimination, others comparatively little; some indicate powerful emotional feeling, others rather less; some remarks are weighted more towards the descriptive end of the spectrum, others towards the evaluative. Moreover in philosophical accounts of the aesthetic a number of apparently paradoxical elements is apt to recur. For it is widely held to be, on the one hand, 'out of this world', on the other, to be part and parcel of it – gratuitous, but constituting an important dimension of human life and often having a profound effect on us. We may be 'taken out of ourselves', yet become more deeply, or perhaps differently, aware of ourselves; aesthetic awareness may involve an introduction to what is strange and new, but also a realisation (in the particular sense discussed above) of what is familiar and seemingly commonplace – even the most homely, everyday things can become the object of such awareness. We can seek aesthetic enjoyment deliberately, but at times it may seem to come upon us unbidden. Beauty in particular, Sircello suggests, is typically what he calls an attention-getter: 'We seem powerless before its pull. It seems as if it is not we who give our attention to beauty, but beauty that, as it were, forces our attention on it'.[1] On the one hand we surrender ourselves to the object of aesthetic contemplation, approaching it in a receptive, open fashion; on the other we keep a certain distance from it, maintaining a critical, alert stance that is never, however, aloof or cold. Our freedom to imagine, to interpret, to create and re-create is in aesthetic appreciation stimulated and expanded, but at the same time – at any rate, in art – restrained and partly held in check.

Some of these ways of referring to aesthetic experience may be of a phenomenological rather than a logical nature. But at rock bottom there usually lies a recognition of the *imaginative* dimension of this mode of awareness that I have maintained is a central feature. There is often, too, recognition of its subjective, yet at the same time objective, character – subjective in that the individual is directly and intimately involved in what he attends to, experiencing feelings of satisfaction or else distaste; objective in the sense that what engages his attention is something in the public world that can be regarded by others as he regards it, and that is, moreover, susceptible to appraisal and checking by means of shared experience and reason-giving. It is the nature of this checking process – in other words, the justifying of aesthetic appraisals – to which we must turn next.

---

[1] *A New Theory of Beauty*, p. 20.

CHAPTER EIGHT

Justifying aesthetic appraisals

It is precisely over matters of taste that men are most prone to argue.

Roger Scruton: 'Architectural taste'.

Before we come to grips with the question of how aesthetic appraisals are to be justified, it may be as well to remind ourselves that, apart from a very few words – and even here there can be ambiguities – there is none that can be considered to have specifically aesthetic force. Rather, as we saw in Chapter 6, words and phrases are 'transposed' (in Schaper's term) from a variety of other spheres of discourse to be *used* aesthetically.

Neither is there a distinctively grammatical form of aesthetic remark. On the contrary, such remarks often share the structure of *statements* and are superficially indistinguishable from them; that is, they appear to state what is the case. Even exclamations, which it is sometimes suggested are more directly expressive of aesthetic experience than statements,[1] imply or perhaps constitute, as Meager points out, elliptically expressed statements: 'How beautiful!', for instance, is to all intents and purposes the equivalent of 'How beautiful that is!', which in turn amounts to 'That is beautiful' ('Aesthetic concepts', p. 305).

It is, of course, fairly obvious that someone is not using terms literally or within their normal sphere of application – and may well be evidencing an aesthetic response – if he speaks of, say, a painting as vigorous or dynamic, a musical work as playful or sparkling, a mountain or a building as noble or threatening: paintings cannot move, music, mountains and buildings do not have moods or moral virtues (or vices). Nevertheless he does seem to be stating a fact; and if he says that a dance is graceful or grotesque this sounds even more like an information-bearing utterance, comparable with an assertion such as that it is syncopated or symmetrically structured. But aesthetic remarks, it has been maintained in preceding chapters, do *not* state facts and are not made independently of the speaker's personal response to something; rather, they have a strongly subjective character in the sense that they reveal something of how he takes it, how it strikes him. While seeming to apply straightforwardly to the object of attention, they indicate also the way he regards it, or, as we might say, his regard *for* it. This is to repeat the point that the aesthetically involved

---

[1] See, for instance, Wittgenstein, L., *Lectures and Conversations on Aesthetics*, I, 9, p. 3.

individual is not engaged in a form of enquiry; he does not, as Elliott rightly insists, approach an artwork (say) like a map,[1] seeking to discern or recognise features that can be known in advance.

A speaker then is 'in' his aesthetic remarks in a way that is not the case with the factual statements he makes. Yet it is not insignificant that they often resemble statements. Indeed this resemblance points to an important feature of aesthetic appraisals and brings us at once to the question of their justification. For to say that something is beautiful, hideous, aesthetically moving, etc., while not constituting a claim to propositional knowledge, is nonetheless – if it is a genuine aesthetic appraisal – an implicit claim that, in Kant's words, 'we can presuppose its validity for all men' (*Critique of Judgement*, s. 6). That is, an aesthetic judgment is not the expression of a personal preference, as in the case of a remark about liking or disliking certain food or certain bodily or movement sensations, but admits of vindication. In this respect, therefore, an aesthetic appraisal is *not* subjective, but has a fundamentally normative character.

It need hardly be pointed out that in fact the agreement of others is not always or even typically or frequently forthcoming. Nor would it settle matters if this were the case. For it has to be, not a contingent, but a logical feature of aesthetic appraisals that they command the assent of others. Thus, as Kant puts it:

> The judgment of taste does not *postulate* the agreement of everyone . . . ; it only *imputes* this agreement to everyone. . . . (s. 8).

The tacit assumption is that what *we* find aesthetically exciting or boring, for example, for all that this is apt to sound as if it might be a report on some causal effect the object has on our mental state, would be the experience of *anyone*: we are ascribing qualities to something external to ourselves that are available to others to experience similarly. This is not, of course, to suggest that someone who says 'That's a pretty dress!', or such like, is always precisely aware of making such a claim, much less that he could always be articulate in trying to justify it. But even when we are unable to provide reasons, we feel that there *are* reasons, that we are not making a mistake.

Hence it is entirely unremarkable that we should be asked *why* we find something lovely, ugly, and so forth – to say more about what we feel *makes* it so; whereas normally it would be strange to be asked why we refer, say, to a gesture as smooth or undulating, a stage as dark or dim, a dancer as a tall blonde or a diminutive redhead (mentioning, that is, first-order features). The question 'Why?', which an aesthetic appraisal not only permits, but typically prompts, thus requires an answer or a reaction of a kind quite different from that we

[1] Cf. 'The critic and the lover of art', pp. 122 and 147.

should make if our judgments about, for instance, texture or shape, colour or size, were challenged. For in those circumstances a request for reasons *in virtue of which* something is smooth, undulating, etc. would be totally out of place: all we could do would be to try to improve conditions for observation – placing the object in a better light, removing possible causes of optical illusion, perhaps – or weighing, measuring, and so forth.

Again, as Michael Weston points out in his paper 'How can we be moved by the fate of Anna Karenina?' we do not in the ordinary course of events ask someone why he is moved by the news of the death of a friend's son: the mere intimation of such a fact is enough. In aesthetic matters, however, it is never an indication of misunderstanding to ask for reasons for a particular response. Indeed a good deal of aesthetic discussion, especially in respect of works of art, consists in providing, or attempting to provide, just this sort of articulation. Moreover what is required by way of reply is not a causal explanation, some account, for example, of the mood or state of health of the person concerned, but reasons – and reasons that are not only appropriate and convincing in his case, but in anyone's. It is part of the logic of an *aesthetic* appraisal that others besides the speaker should not only respond as he does, but for the same reasons.

However the giving of reasons here does not, as in deductive reasoning (in proving, for instance, that the angles of a triangle total 180 degrees), consist of a step-by-step argument which leads from a given premise to an inescapable conclusion. It consists, rather, in getting another person to see the point of an appraisal, where 'seeing the point', somewhat as with seeing a joke, involves his coming to have a similar view of the object, and, with that, a similar felt response. To justify an aesthetic appraisal is thus to justify its acceptance; and the criterion for his acceptance is that particular experience of delight (or distaste) consequent upon the act of imaginative attention that it was a principal aim of the previous chapter to elucidate. Such justification, therefore, unlike the justifying of moral or religious utterances (of which it might also be said that the speaker is 'in' his words), has a sensory as well as an affective and intellectual dimension. It requires the bringing about of 'communication at the level of the senses', in Arnold Isenberg's phrase: the speaker's meaning is ' "filled in", "rounded out", or "completed" by the act of perception'. And this act is performed not to judge the truth of the description, but to *understand* it.[1]

To try to justify an aesthetic appraisal, then, the person making it will describe the object *as it appears to him* and point out what *makes* it, say, exhilarating or comic or banal. His further description(s) are descriptions of what he is responding to: the *intentional* object. If he characterised this differently he would convey a different experience. His task therefore, which is also, as Stanley Cavell pertinently observes, that of the artist, is

---

[1] 'Critical communication', pp. 137–138, as reprinted in (ed.) W. Elton, *Aesthetics and Language*.

not to discount his subjectivity, but to include it; not to overcome it in agreement, but to master it in exemplary ways (*Must We Mean What We Say?*, p. 94).

And for the person who (successfully) follows the speaker's suggestions to 'Look at (or listen to) it this way. . . .', perception and response are simultaneously changed: the object or performance becomes, for example, exhilarating (or comic or banal, etc.) for him too. It is for this reason that the procedure and its result are often compared with that phenomenon discussed at length by Wittgenstein in the second part of the *Philosophical Investigations* in connection with 'seeing as' and what he calls the 'dawning of an aspect':

> Not only can you give a new description of it, but noticing the second figure was a new visual experience (p. 199e).

(This discussion, it should be noted, relates to a number of highly diverse as well as highly problematic philosophical issues, but is conducted – perhaps not altogether helpfully, since it introduces additional complexities[1] – chiefly in terms of ambiguous figures such as the Jastrow duck-rabbit.) It is not then as if a better view were obtained of something that was previously seen only dimly or partially, as when a screen is removed or a light switched on;[2] what we experience as we look or listen or read again is totally different.

The contrast between aesthetic and merely sensuous awareness is thus once more markedly apparent; for we should hardly expect to *reason* someone into (or out of) liking or disliking a scent, a flavour, a movement sensation, etc. Such experiences do not usually alter as a result of description or re-description, or reference to what Wollheim calls 'sustaining features' (such as first-order properties). Indeed there is very little, if anything, to which one can call attention in respect of finding pleasure (or otherwise) in, say, the aroma or taste of coffee, or the sensation of turning a somersault or being lifted high above the ground: it is not as if some detail had been overlooked here to which attention could be directed. Neither is it possible for an individual to try to see or hear something *as* it in fact *is*. It makes no sense to say, for instance, 'Now see this group as kneeling in a circle' or 'Try to see that dancer's fingers as spread out' (as distinct from *noticing* such things). But it does make sense, and may be very helpful, to suggest that if he notices how the zig-zag floor patterns of a dance contrast with the rounded or spiralling gestures of the dancers, for example, he

---

[1] See Wollheim, R., *Art and Its Objects*, pp. 219–220.
[2] Cf. Strawson, P. F., 'Wittgenstein's *Philosophical Investigations*', p. 163ff. (as reprinted in *Freedom and Resentment*).

may become aware of a note of dramatic tension – or, in another context, a bizarre or perhaps comic quality – breaking in on the previous calm, harmonious mood.

In other words, whereas ordinary perception *cannot* be brought about imaginatively or at will, aesthetic appreciation is an imaginative *achievement* involving what Wittgenstein, in his discussion of seeing a picture of a triangle as a picture of a fallen pyramid, calls 'the mastery of a technique' (*Philosophical Investigations*, p. 208e). Aesthetic interest is thus something that can be aided and developed by practice and education. (There are also, of course, several other 'techniques' to do with *ordinary* perception that may help aesthetic awareness – for instance, switching attention rapidly back and forth between small points of interest and the wider 'scene', focusing on, say, details of a dancer's footwork, then scanning the whole stage to take in groupings and such like.)

There can, however, be no logical guarantee of success on the part of someone making an aesthetic judgment who then tries to bring another to share his experience. For, since there is no entailment relation between the first-order features of an object and its aesthetic qualities, there may be, and indeed often are, rival interpretations. This is especially likely with works of art, which are often of a highly complex character – 'many-levelled', 'multi-layered', 'many-faceted like a jewel', as they are regularly described. They may therefore present different aspects to different individuals, or even to the same individual on different occasions; and not only may further qualities become evident of which he had not been previously aware, but these may conflict with those that had earlier been apparent. What, for example, once seemed merely frivolous may now be seen as grimly humorous or bitingly satirical; what was formerly charming or rich may now seem emotionally indulgent or lush.

An important contrast is to be noted here with the so-called clicking-on and -off effect of the differing aspects of ambiguous figures such as the duck-rabbit; for whereas we can switch from one to another and back in these cases, we are unlikely ever to experience again as charming what we now find sentimental. For one thing, additional knowledge and understanding may have been acquired which cannot, as it were, be suspended when we return to the object, see the dance, play, film, or whatever at a later date. Such further experience may, of course, include increased knowledge of the arts and greater aesthetic sensitivity generally. As Casey puts it:

> evolving aesthetic preferences is something like being led unsuspectingly into a trap which closes behind one. . . . You cannot decide to jettison great areas of moral and aesthetic knowledge at will any more than you can decide to forget what you know about mathematics or history (*The Language of Criticism*, p. 24).

At this point it may be useful to consider how an individual's reappraisal of something, or an enrichment of his original view, may come about, for this may be effected in a variety of ways.

In the first place, he may come to see it in a new light unaided (unaided, at any rate, at that moment: he is always to some extent indebted to others, as with any form of understanding). He may, for instance, become aware of certain aspects previously overlooked simply by spending more time watching, say, a film loop of a dance sequence, or by reading or performing a piece (or an extract) over and over again, perhaps in the last case trying out such things as a change of tempo or dynamics. In this connection we should not forget the possible importance of information external to the work or object itself – the individual's 'cognitive stock' – as discussed in earlier chapters. Some understanding of Greek myth, for example, can alter perception and appreciation of many of Graham's dances (not always favourably); while knowing that a composer was aware of his impending death can bring an added poignancy to the experience of a particular work – as, notably, with Mozart's *Requiem* and Schubert's *Death and the Maiden Quartet* (with that 'dance of death' quality of the Finale); and as would appear to have been the case with many who saw Limón's *The Unsung*.[1] It is also possible to find illumination – though sometimes puzzlement – in clues given by the artist: the dedication of a work, say, or its title (e.g. Carl Nielsen's *Inextinguishable Symphony*, Glen Tetley's *Embrace Tiger and Return to Mountain*).

Often, however, it is from the more mature aesthetic responses of others that we gain fresh perspectives – typically conveyed, in the case of a skilled 'guide', by means of a rich vocabulary, which may perhaps include a judicious use of simile and metaphor. It is not only *what* he says, however, that may prove telling, but also his manner of saying it (tone of voice, gestures, etc.);[2] he might also hum, dance or act excerpts from a work. Technical and semi-technical terms appropriate to the art form under discussion or to objects such as boats or pieces of furniture have a useful role, too, in enabling someone to understand an aesthetic appraisal inasmuch as they make it possible to refer to quite specific details. The importance of attention to detail, both for profitable debate about aesthetically interesting objects and for their fuller appreciation can, indeed, hardly be exaggerated. For an awareness of even seemingly trivial nuances can make for new or modified perceptions and responses, and the subtler and more highly differentiated the details selected and, as it were, woven together, the more complete and convincing a picture may be built up by any individual seeking to justify his claim.

Only if certain distinctions can be recognised, then – in dance, the difference

---

[1] See Jowitt, D., *Dance Beat*, pp. 93–94.

[2] Cf. Sibley, F. N., 'Aesthetic and non-aesthetic', s.III, and 'Aesthetic concepts', s.II.

between a sliding step and an ordinary step, a gesture 'led' by the little finger edge of the hand rather than the back of the wrist, a variation on a theme by means of inversion, etc. – can certain appraisals be understood. And understanding here, it should perhaps be emphasised again, involves not merely knowing *that* this part is the first variation (or the introduction, the development section, or whatever), but *experiencing* it as such. Accurate reference to movement details, it may also be added, is importantly linked, as in the case of music, with the availability of an adequate system of notation (which is all too often regarded simply as a useful means of preserving dances, rather than as facilitating appreciation in distinctively kinetic terms). Drawing attention to details to do with lighting, props, costumes and, of course, sound accompaniment may also make important differences to someone's appraisal – or reappraisal – of a dance work or a particular performance of it.

In the case of the performing arts new ways of 'taking' either a complete work or particular passages, characters, situations, etc. are offered by different performances and productions; indeed they *are* new ways of taking them. Hence the importance of not identifying a *work* with any single presentation or interpreter (difficult though this sometimes is in practice – as, presumably, for her contemporaries in the classic case of Anna Pavlova and the *Dying Swan*). Moreover even an individual performing his own composition is likely to give a slightly different, possibly significantly different, rendering on subsequent occasions.

There is in fact a certain similarity between the activity of the performing artist and that of the critic, since each is concerned, albeit by very different means and in differing degrees, with bringing out the meaning(s) of a work, with interpreting, or reinterpreting, it. And here it is worth noting Schaper's mention of the German word *auslegen* in this context, 'to lay out from within', which conveys the sense of selecting, collecting and gathering together, as contrasted with *interpretieren*, 'to act as a go-between' (*Prelude to Aesthetics*, p. 138).

However, a particular presentation is itself subject to differing appraisals, and here again the connoisseur may open up new ways of seeing or hearing as he calls attention to, for instance, the interplay in a concerto between the soloist and orchestra, so that we hear it in *this* rendering less as an argumentative dialogue, say, than as an amiable conversation. But it is not always by exclusive reference to the work or object in question that changes of response may occur: we often become aware of particular nuances, or even its overall character, by means of comparisons and contrasts with other works and objects.

Furthermore, what may enable someone to provide a satisfying answer to the (aptly-worded) question, 'What do you see in it?' is knowledge and experience of art forms other than the one under discussion, or of things commonly regarded as aesthetically valuable such as Japanese and Chinese calligraphy, scrolls, fans, etc. This is hardly surprising, for in seeking to appreciate more fully an artwork in its particularity, we typically relate one piece to another and, in so doing, as Wollheim points out, build up a more complete picture of art itself (*Art and Its Objects*, pp. 198–199).

Such breadth of experience, as well as depth of understanding of particular works, is often enriched too by knowledge both of art history and of the body of critical literature belonging to the various art forms. For although, as Elliott argues, it can happen in the arts, as in other disciplines, that a critical tradition may prove cramping, it is a powerful instrument of freedom;[1] it enables us to entertain new interpretations and yet to resist contemporary cults and fashions. And so it might be suggested that the grave disadvantages from which the dance suffers in the absence of a substantial corpus of criticism (to which attention has already been drawn) might to some extent be reduced by study of critical texts in, say, music and drama. Indeed, not only may these be of assistance in a general way (as well as interesting, of course, in their own right), but music criticism in particular may be of direct value in the appreciation and evaluation of dances inspired by musical works (as, for example, with most of George Balanchine's compositions).

Nevertheless it cannot be insisted too strongly that what we are considering in this chapter is the justifying of a felt response, not of a belief or a theoretical hypothesis. Learning *about* a work of art, therefore, either from other people or books, etc., cannot by itself lead to *aesthetic* appraisal: it is always against not merely observable, but actually observed, features of an object that such an appraisal has to be tested. Thus, while the views of cultured and scholarly individuals might normally be expected to prove worth endeavouring to share, the responses of the less erudite – those who do not suffer, in Tanner's phrase, from a hardening of the aesthetic arteries[2] – can sometimes be just as valuable. For in this sphere it is not a matter of 'If we go on looking at and listening to and studying X long enough, someone is bound eventually to arrive at an indisputable conclusion': there *cannot* be any such conclusion.

Nor is the creative artist in a more unassailable position than anyone else, though this does not mean, of course, that there is nothing to be gained from what a choreographer, a potter, a film director and so on might say about either his work in general or a particular piece. It would indeed be foolish (as well as presumptuous) not to heed whatever a creative artist might care to tell us about what he is doing or trying to do, what sort of approach to his work would be appropriate or inappropriate, and so forth, especially in cases where there is a radical departure from established practices and traditions. Yet it is always possible, first, that not only might he be too involved with whatever he has achieved to be able suitably to distance himself from it, and hence adequately to appraise it, but other people might be capable of a more just appreciation as a

[1] 'Education, love of one's subject, and the love of truth', p. 140.

[2] 'Objectivity and aesthetics', p. 71.

result of being able to place his work within a broader cultural and historical perspective or of possessing knowledge that he does not have. Secondly, it is possible for the artist to fail in his intentions; for while these are sometimes indicated in, say, letters or diaries, they are ultimately identifiable by reference to the work itself.

There might then be either more or less in a particular piece than the artist intended or could have intended (consider, for example, Freudian interpretations of *Othello* or some of Leonardo da Vinci's works). Moreover later generations have certain benefits of hindsight: they are necessarily in a position to be able to bring to artworks from the past knowledge that was not available at the time to the artist or to his contemporary critics, but that sometimes facilitate new and interesting interpretations. On the other hand information is often lacking that would be helpful – perhaps is even necessary – for appreciating properly some aspects of certain artworks of earlier times (it is not known, for instance, precisely how Mediaeval plainsong was phrased and rhythmicised[1]).

However it does not follow from the fact that a particular object of aesthetic interest may bear a variety of interpretations, some of them quite irreconcilable, that *any* will do. On the contrary, somewhat as with ambiguous figures, 'pictures' in the fire, clouds, stained walls, and the like (though the analogy cannot be pressed very far), there are some interpretations that are not merely implausible, but *wrong*. Anyone, for example, who found Robert Cohan's *Cell* a comic, light-hearted dance would simply be mistaken: he would have failed to understand the work. Similarly, to see Iago riding on Othello's back in *The Moor's Pavane* as an amusing, good-humoured episode, would be a failure to grasp its sinister and deeply symbolic import. In the aesthetic situation, in contrast to situations of fantasy and reverie, imagination is not entirely free but is restrained and controlled by the structure of whatever is the object of attention – an object, that is, with features that are open to public scrutiny.

The significance of such constraints, however, is often ignored or not even recognised by those who are apt to be over-impressed by the range of contrasting aesthetic appraisals that a particular artwork (or other object) may be able to sustain. Furthermore there is often a failure to appreciate that genuine disagreement can occur only in areas in which there is the possiblity of agreement: people do not enter into dispute over matters in which the question of standards is absurd. If one person enjoys the motion of a rolling ship, for instance, and another does not, that is all there is to it; it does not make sense to try to argue about it, i.e. about a sensation. Neither agreement nor disagreement has any point in such cases. Differences between individuals in respect of objects of aesthetic interest, by contrast, *are* genuine disagreements: they presuppose the existence of norms, even though the disputants may not be precisely aware of this, and even though – to reiterate a point already emphasised several times in previous chapters – there is not, and cannot be, any fixed body of absolute criteria to which appeal can be made.

Sometimes a certain measure of agreement is easily recognised. For example, while someone might say that a dance was profoundly moving which another found merely touching, both would at least be agreeing that it was not lacking warmth – rather as (to use an over-simplified analogy) there might be a difference of opinion as to whether a person was smirking or simpering or genuinely smiling, but no question that he might be scowling. If, however, *no* common ground between two disputants is at first to be found, then it may be possible to reach agreement by means of appropriate comparisons with something else: 'Well, *that* is a neatly rounded, balanced piece, wouldn't you say? Now notice the number of loose ends in *this* one – how a new idea is introduced here – and here – and here, but never comes to anything as far as I can see, isn't related to anything else in it. That's why I say it's richly inventive but is a sprawling, bitty affair'. Further, a good deal of agreement in aesthetic matters is of a fundamental kind, and for this very reason apt to be obscured by its existing at a level at which certain shared attitudes and values are so much taken for granted that it is hardly ever necessary to refer to them. It is at that level where, for instance, it is in general tacitly agreed as a starting point for discussion that, over a wide range of cases, certain things *are* works of art, and that foremost among these are the masterpieces of, say, Shakespeare, Bach and Michelangelo.

Nevertheless, since disagreement in the aesthetic realm is often more striking and obvious than agreement, the view remains widespread – not least, unhappily, among some closely concerned with the arts and with aesthetic values in general – that 'It's all a matter of taste' ('taste' here indicating merely personal predilections, as in that sphere in which the term has its natural home, namely to do with what one likes to eat and drink). Yet such a view is rarely borne out by other aspects of the behaviour of those who may unreflectively give voice to it. For whereas a difference in taste for, say, garlic does not typically generate discussion about whose preference is the more *intelligible* or can be regarded as rational or irrational, most individuals seem ready to leap to the defence of their views on the aesthetic merits of, for example, a car, an item of dress, where a picture should hang in a room, and, not least, pictures themselves, dances, and so on. (Whether that defence is articulate or inarticulate, convincing or confused, is of course a further question.) To continue Scruton's further remarks following that with which this chapter began:

> Anger is expressed at the erection of a sky-scraper in Paris or a shopping precinct in some quiet Cathedral town, and this anger is quite incompatible with the assumption that in matters of taste dispute is pointless, that each man has the right to his own opinion, that nothing is objective, nothing right or wrong ('Architectural taste', p. 294).

A visit to the theatre characteristically confirms this. For members of an audience are usually interested (say, during an interval or at the end of the performance) not only in expressing *their* reactions to a work and/or its presentation, but also in finding out about the reactions of others; and not merely in terms of how they rate it, but why – why they say it is trite, powerful, amusing, and so on. Moreover in critical discussion we seek to persuade, and are ourselves persuaded (when we *are* persuaded), not by a process of deductive reasoning but in ways which, to make the point again, result in modified perception, and with that a change of felt response.

That such a procedure is to count as *reasoning*, even when conducted systematically and skilfully – as by an experienced professional critic – is, however, sometimes denied. Sibley, for example, argues at some length in the last part of 'Aesthetic and non-aesthetic' that 'an activity the successful outcome of which is seeing or hearing cannot . . . be called reasoning'; though he allows that if someone gets others to see the aesthetic qualities he sees, this may be called '*a* way of supporting or justifying, even of proving, an aesthetic judgment' – and, moreover, tellingly illustrates just this sort of procedure, referring to it as 'perceptual proof'.

Now, clearly, any suggestion that the justification of an aesthetic appraisal consists in deriving a logically unassailable conclusion from a certain premise, as in deductive argument, is as wholly out of place as the suggestion that what are needed here are the inductive methods of the physical sciences. (In both cases this would mean that someone could establish the aesthetic character of something without ever coming face to face with it himself.) But to set up the model of deductive reasoning, where the conclusion is a thought involving belief, as the *only* type of sound reasoning there is, is unduly restrictive. Indeed if, as Scruton puts it, a process that has as its endpoint an experience rather than a judgment is not reasoning, what is? For though not involving belief, the experience in question (unlike ordinary perception), is subject to the will, an achievement resulting from a particular kind of attention, and it does not seem inappropriate, therefore, to consider such an achievement the conclusion of a process of reasoning.[1]

It might, however, be asked whether it really matters that aesthetic disagreements persist. Given the immense diversity of human beings and the extraordinary variety of phenomena that characteristically evoke aesthetic interest, is there not something to be said, it might be suggested, for *not* seeking to persuade or be persuaded in this realm? Certainly some philosophers have taken the view that such differences between people are not only to be expected,

[1] *The Aesthetics of Architecture*, chs. 5 and 10. (The above is a very condensed summary of an intricate but, in my view, compelling argument.)

but welcomed. Hungerland, for instance, claims that she is delighted rather than distressed:

> In moral matters, we must achieve some large measure of agreement or be annihilated. In science, we must require agreement or abandon the project . . . . In art, we can be out of step with the rest of the world without endangering a single soul or abandoning the enterprise. How delightful![1]

Kennick writes in remarkably similar terms in his paper 'Does traditional aesthetics rest on a mistake?'.

Such a stance, however, seems to involve the assumption that aesthetic interest has no connection with our other interests and concerns. Yet although the aesthetic is non-practical in character (in the sense discussed in the previous chapter), it does not follow that it is any less fundamental to or significant in our lives than moral, scientific or legal matters, and so on; nor that it can be completely hived off from the rest of our ideals and standards. On the contrary, what an individual finds exciting, moving, outrageous, amusing and so forth about, say, a dance, is ultimately not to be divorced from his beliefs about what is admirable, trivial, deplorable, tragic and so on in life generally. His aesthetic responses, that is, are continuous with his social, ethical, religious, political, and other values. Thus aesthetic appraisals in respect of the arts, natural phenomena, houses, gardens, dress and other aspects of personal appearance, etc. reflect what we find important in life; though experience of such things – the literature we read, the dances, sculptures, buildings, scenes that we look at, and so forth – is capable of leading us to reconsider and sometimes modify those ideals and values. For there is here a two-way flow: what might be called a 'vision of life' enters into and at the same time is partly constituted by our aesthetic encounters.[2] Our aesthetic responses are one way in which our attempts to make sense of the world and our experience of living is revealed; and a change in other areas of thought and feeling does not leave our aesthetic sensibilities untouched.

Nowhere is this better illustrated than in relation to the dance. Indeed differences in the appeal of traditional classical ballet as contrasted with much modern dance, of acrobatic or tap-dancing as contrasted with dance as a fine art, of ballroom or 'disco' dancing, and so forth, would seem to be as much moral as they are aesthetic (even if the nature of the appeal is not precisely recognised for what it is by those who participate or watch). It is not merely that the subject matter of much theatre dance, as well as what originally prompted a good many folk dances, has to do with human situations and con-

---

[1] 'Once again, aesthetic and non-aesthetic', p. 111 (as reprinted in (ed.) H. Osborne, *Aesthetics*).
[2] Cf. Weston, M., 'How can we be moved by the fate of Anna Karenina?', pp. 92–93.

cerns; but in abstract works too, and in fact in all dancing, some conception of what a human being is like is implicit in whatever is performed. For the dance, simply by virtue of its medium – the movement of human beings – reveals something of human capabilities and limitations, aspirations and weaknesses, and, of course, certain attitudes towards the body, including how it is to be treated and 'displayed'.

Thus if a dancer constantly grovels on the floor, slithers along on his stomach like a snake, or runs about on all fours, this might be one thing in a representational dance but is likely to be quite another in an abstract piece. To move in a Caliban-like manner, as distinct from dancing the role of Caliban, implicitly – or maybe explicitly – presents a picture of the human being with a mentality quite different from that apparent when a dancer is always soaring and floating above the ground in a seemingly effortless, ethereal manner. Similarly, attitudes towards the sexes are often strikingly revealed in the dances of various cultures, expectations and ideals as regards male and female dancers differing radically in some, in others much less so.[1]

It is not so much a question then of whether aesthetic concerns are as important as moral concerns, as whether a developed aesthetic sense can ultimately be divorced from a moral sense. This, it perhaps should be pointed out, is to take 'moral' not in the narrow sense of relating only to duty, right or wrong action and conduct, but as having to do also with ideals, character, and the cultivation of mind.[2] A sense of the *appropriate*, as exemplified in aesthetic discrimination, may indeed be regarded, as Scruton urges, as one of the most important areas of practical reason – though one that he claims is apt to be neglected in moral philosophy. Moreover without a sense of what is appropriate in the aesthetic sphere, he further argues, it is possible that our sense of what is right and wrong 'will itself be inexorably eroded'.[3]

'It's all a matter of taste' is thus a view that not only is misleading inasmuch as it implies that there is nothing more to be said when someone offers an aesthetic appraisal, but is based on the false assumption that the justification of such appraisals is an isolated matter. Rather, what is involved is a complex network of beliefs, convictions, and feelings as to 'what life is about', what is worth striving for and preserving or rejecting. It is precisely because our aesthetic preferences tie in so closely with what matters most to us, Scruton goes on to suggest, that we are drawn into a quest for aesthetic standards and seem, even in the face of persistent disappointment, constrained to pursue an ideal of objectivity.

It is, of course, especially in connection with the arts that deep and sometimes

[1] Cf. Pauly, H., 'Inside Kabuki: an experience in comparative aesthetics', p. 300ff; see also my 'Aesthetic qualities in the dance and their significance in education', pp. 238–241.
[2] Cf. Diffey, T. J., 'Morality and literary criticism'.
[3] 'Architectural taste', pp. 327–328; see also his *The Aesthetics of Architecture*, chs. 5, 9 and 10.

bitter aesthetic disagreements are most evident – partly, perhaps, because critical argument, in the case of most art forms, at any rate, is carried on systematically at a professional level, is published and itself reviewed, as well as often studied in conjunction with appreciation of the works in question (it is, as we have seen, a vital part of the institutional framework within which art is situated). And it is hardly surprising that what particularly provoke heated debate are works of art which themselves treat of human ambitions, ideals and passions, as notably in the case of much of Wagner's music. For what is at issue here, as Tanner points out in 'Objectivity and aesthetics', is the moral desirability of living at such an extreme level of emotional intensity. Similar considerations have been raised in connection with some of Wigman's compositions, Lincoln Kirstein, for example, writing of her dancing as 'that assertion of blind, vague, quasi-mystical self-expressionism which is the unfortunate universal heritage of the descent from Wagner'.[1]

What is usually under review when the justification of aesthetic appraisals is discussed is, of course, what people *say* about works of art and other objects occasioning an aesthetic response. But it would be wrong to suppose that such appreciation is revealed and expressed only through words. 'This is beautiful', typically regarded as the prototype of an aesthetic judgment, not only is but one of a number of things an individual might say about something he admires aesthetically; it is but one of a number of things he might do. Wittgenstein, discussing a related point in his *Lectures and Conversations on Aesthetics, etc.*, says:

> What are expressions of liking something? Is it only what we say or interjections we use or faces we make? Obviously not. It is, often, how often I read something or how often I wear a suit. Perhaps I won't even say: 'It's fine', but wear it often and look at it (I, 6, p. 12).

Similarly, aesthetic sensitivity might be indicated by the way a person holds himself, walks, and moves about generally; by his manner of addressing another individual, and by the objects with which he surrounds himself; by his going to see a particular dance or film whenever the opportunity presents itself; applauding or shouting enthusiastically after a performance; and so forth. In other words, by what Wittgenstein, in the *Philosophical Investigations*, calls 'fine shades of behaviour': his understanding of a musical theme, for instance, may be, as he puts it, 'expressed by my whistling it with the correct expression' (p. 207e). Alternatively, refraining from doing certain things, avoiding certain activities and objects, walking out of a performance, etc. might constitute an aesthetic response.

[1] In (ed.) M. Armitage, *Martha Graham*, p. 27.

In contrast to some action or activity, however, there is the possible significance of stillness and silence. Indeed this would seem to be a common reaction in cases where the experience is especially powerful. One might, for instance, be struck dumb by beauty, by the horror or pity of a work of art, by brilliance, magnificence or deep expressiveness; and to speak at once, let alone engage in detailed conversation, following the performance of, say, a profoundly moving dance or a piece of music could be totally inappropriate. Moreover, as Sircello points out, the beauties we commonly encounter are often so fleeting that many people do not want to risk spoiling the experience by talking about it (*A New Theory of Beauty*, p. 119).

But of course silence and stillness are not necessarily evidence of *aesthetic* interest, even in the presence of what might generally be agreed is a great work of art or (say) a scene of great natural beauty. For such behaviour is compatible with an attitude of curiosity, religious or mystical awe, admiration of skill, or even indifference. In the absence of further behaviour it is impossible to tell. In contrast then to flower arranging, decorating a cake, or performing a dance in particular ways, something more is necessary on the part of, for example, someone gazing silently at a sunrise or listening in complete stillness to music, if his interest is to be identified as aesthetic. And this 'something more' must express the person's conception of what he is attending to, how it comes across to him, so to speak. In other words the *imaginative* dimension of his experience must be made apparent.

In such cases, therefore, it would seem that the need for words cannot be avoided. For it to be established that his pleasure (or distaste) is rooted in an aesthetic appraisal, the individual has to say something about the object he is looking at or listening to which will count as an aesthetic remark – some utterance that can be justified by appropriate reasons. Further, the sort of non-verbal behaviour mentioned earlier as possible expressions of aesthetic discernment – wearing a particular item of clothing or jewellery, applauding or withholding applause after a dance performance, etc. – is only a very general manifestation of appreciation: it may amount to little more than an expression of liking or disliking of a rather undifferentiated kind. Although prompted by a particular object or event, such behaviour does not express a particular appraisal; and, again, more is required in order for it to be established how precisely the object or event is viewed.

Thus a strong indication of aesthetic appreciation is that a person can use a range of terms and expressions in such a way as to reveal how the object strikes him, his regard for it, and not just words such as 'lovely' and 'fine', which, though often having aesthetic force, are apt to be used somewhat indiscriminately and imprecisely.[1] On the other hand, what someone might say – or in some cases

[1] For a detailed examination of commonly used terms in the aesthetic appreciation of dance, see my 'Aesthetic qualities in the dance and their significance in education', ch. 5.

do – that *seems* to reveal aesthetic appreciation might not be a sincere response. For he might have learned (e.g. by watching and listening to others) how to make the 'right' moves or noises,[1] yet not be *in* his words or deeds – rather as someone might laugh when others laugh at a joke, yet fail to be amused.

This raises the question of how a genuine aesthetic response is to be distinguished from either one that is feigned or one the true character of which is misunderstood by the experiencing individual himself. For it is possible in relation to aesthetic matters, no less than to any others, to deceive both other people and oneself. An individual might, indeed, make a show of a response he did not really feel for a variety of reasons. And while on the one hand his experience might be genuinely aesthetic yet he might disguise its precise details, on the other it might not be aesthetic at all. In both cases there would seem no sure-fire way of another finding out the truth, though over a period of time certain traits, ambitions, pretensions, motives, etc. might become apparent in such a way as to justify suspicion about that person's aesthetic sensibilities, especially if there were also a lack of sincerity evident in other departments of his life and a general tendency on his part to exhibit shallowness of feeling or little capacity for independent thought.

The idea that we may deceive ourselves, however, either as regards what are our actual feelings or what is their source or object, may strike some people as strange; and the suggestion that we are not always the best – and certainly not the only – 'authority' on our own state of mind is often unwelcome. Yet it is clear that there *are* occasions, not least those involving the arts and aesthetic experience more generally, when we can be shown to be mistaken in this respect, when others know better than we do ourselves about both our mental state and what accounts for it. Thus it is possible to discover, for example, that what we had earlier believed to be *aesthetically* enjoyable or repulsive was the source of pleasure or displeasure for some quite different reason – for, say, its associations with a certain place, a person, or a period in our life.

This points to the need for a preparedness to examine those responses we suppose to be aesthetic and, partly to aid such examination, regularly to exchange our views with other people. Indeed it may be argued that for anyone to attempt to engage in artistic and aesthetic appreciation, yet to remain unconcerned with cultivating his capacities for discriminating and critical appraisal and for articulating his experience, is not to participate fully in the enterprise. But the implications extend more widely, since the feelings we have about artworks and other objects of aesthetic interest are a vital constituent of, and affect (or infect), our lives as a whole. It is thus hardly less important to try to be aware of what are our feelings in respect of, say, a dance or a musical item than in respect of a person.

[1] Cf. Jones, P., *Philosophy and the Novel*, pp. 201–203, and 'Understanding a work of art', pp. 143–144.

Perhaps what has to be guarded against especially is sentimentality; for if Tanner is right, this is 'a very large ingredient' of disorderly and dull emotional lives. Contrasting it with 'the fulness of emotional vitality', which he takes to be the ideal, Tanner argues that it is characteristic for the sentimentalist 'to inhibit those checking devices which are available, though hard to handle, for interrogating one's experiences'.[1] The feelings that are worth having, he insists, are those which it costs an effort to have (though it is not this that then makes them valuable); and whereas a feature of sentimental feelings is that they are 'easy', easy to come and easy to go, unsentimental emotions are typically deepened and made more secure by pondering and probing. Which is one reason, Tanner adds, why the alleged dichotomy of feeling and thought is so harmful.

Of course an inclination and willingness to join in debate about an artwork, etc. may sometimes, perhaps even often, be lacking. Sircello, discussing beauty, observes that the sort of verbal activity involving analysis and precise description of whatever is under review is just what most people cannot engage in, or cannot engage in well; and he further claims that it is sometimes those who are most sensitive to 'subtle and hard-to-find beauties' who are the least capable and the least willing.[2] One might initially be inclined to sympathise with this suggestion. Yet if such individuals do not make their responses public in some way, it might be asked how they could ever be known to be aesthetically sensitive to the beauties (or other qualities) in question.

This is not to say that one should be expected to arrive at or deliver an 'instant' aesthetic judgment on each and every occasion; but *always* to keep silent, *never* to communicate one's experiences in the aesthetic realm, is to evade a vital moral issue. Moreover however reluctant to express an opinion one might feel, and however difficult it might be to back it up with appropriate reasons, this is something that can be developed and improved with practice, particularly in the company of others more skilled and perceptive than oneself. And inasmuch as each individual stands to gain from sharing responses with other people, this is a further reason for his contributing whatever he can to the discussion of those things in which he believes he takes aesthetic delight or finds aesthetically distasteful.

The ordinary lover of the dance, as well as the professional critic, has a particular responsibility here. For any art form that lacks a lively tradition of critical debate runs the risk of becoming stunted in its development and scope. Indeed, as witness the consequences in totalitarian societies of the repression of art criticism and the censorship of art, the absence of such a tradition threatens artists and their public alike; and this to the detriment of the society as a whole.

[1] 'Sentimentality', p. 134.
[2] *A New Theory of Beauty*, p. 119.

Bibliography

Abbreviations
APQ   *American Philosophical Quarterly*
ASSV   *Aristotelian Society, Supplementary Volume*
BJA   *British Journal of Aesthetics*
JAAC   *Journal of Aesthetics and Art Criticism*
PAS   *Proceedings of the Aristotelian Society*
Phil. Rev. *Philosophical Review*

Abse, D. (1977), *Collected Poems, 1958–76* (London: Hutchinson).

Anscombe, G. E. M. (1958), 'On brute facts', *Analysis*, 18, 69–72.

Aristotle, *Poetics* (translated J. Warrington, London: Dent, 1963).

Armitage, M. (1937), *Martha Graham* (reprinted New York: Dance Horizons, 1968).

Austin, J. L. (1962), *How to do Things with Words* (Oxford: Clarendon Press).

Bambrough, R. (1973), 'To reason is to generalise', *The Listener*, 89, 2285.

Banes, S. (1980), *Terpsichore in Sneakers: Post-Modern Dance* (Boston: Houghton Mifflin).

Barrett, C. (1973), 'Are bad works of art "works of art"?', in *Philosophy and the Arts: Royal Institute of Philosophy Lectures*, Vol. 6 (London: Macmillan).

Beardsley, M. C. (1958), *Aesthetics: Problems in the Philosophy of Criticism* (New York: Harcourt, Brace & World).

Beardsley, M. C. (1969), 'Aesthetic experience regained', *JAAC*, XXVIII, 3–11.

Beardsley, M. C. (1970), *The Possibility of Criticism* (Detroit: Wayne University Press).

Beardsley, M. C. (1970), 'The aesthetic point of view', reprinted in (ed.) J. Margolis, *Philosophy Looks at the Arts* (2nd ed., Philadelphia: Temple University Press).

Beardsley, M. C. and Wimsatt, W. K. (1946), 'The intentional fallacy', reprinted in (ed.) W. K. Wimsatt, *The Verbal Icon* (New York: Noonday, 1966).

Beardsmore, R. W. (1973), 'Two trends in contemporary aesthetics', *BJA*, 13, 346–366.

Bell, C. (1915), *Art* (reprinted, London: Chatto & Windus, 1931).

Best, D. (1974), *Expression in Movement and the Arts* (London: Lepus Books, Henry Kimpton Publishers).

Best, D. (1978), *Philosophy and Human Movement* (London: Allen & Unwin).

Best, D. (1980), 'A policy for the study of physical education and human movement', *Journal of Human Movement Studies*, 6, 336–347.

Best, D. (1982), 'The aesthetic and the artistic', *Philosophy*, 57, 357–372.

Binkley, T. (1976), 'Deciding about art', in (ed.) L. Aagaard-Mogensen, *Culture and Art* (Atlantic Highlands, N. J.: Humanities Press).

Binkley, T. (1977), 'Piece: contra aesthetics', reprinted in (ed.) J. Margolis, *Philosophy Looks at the Arts* (2nd ed.).

Blizek, W. L. (1974), 'An institutional theory of art', *BJA*, 14, 142–150.

Blocker, G. (1980), 'Autonomy, reference and Post-Modern art', *BJA*, 20, 229–236.

Bullough, E. (1912), ' "Psychical distance" as a factor in art and an aesthetic principle', reprinted in (ed.) M. Rader, *A Modern Book of Aesthetics* (3rd ed., New York: Holt, Rinehart & Winston, 1960).

Casey, J. (1966), *The Language of Criticism* (London: Methuen).

Cavell, S. (1976), *Must We Mean What We Say?* (London: CUP).

Chanan, M. (1972), 'Art as experiment', *BJA*, 12, 133–147.

Charlton, W. (1970), *Aesthetics* (London: Hutchinson).

Charlton, W. (1972), 'Aestheticism', *BJA*, 12, 121–132.

Cohen, S. J. (1966), *The Modern Dance: Seven Statements of Belief* (Connecticut: Wesleyan University Press).

Cohen, S. J. (1974), *Dance as a Theatre Art* (London: Harper & Row).

Cohen, T. (1973), 'The possibility of art: remarks on a proposal by Dickie', *Phil. Rev.*, LXXXII, 69–82.

Collingwood, R. G. (1938), *The Principles of Art* (Oxford: Clarendon Press).

Coton, A. V. (1946), *The New Ballet: Kurt Jooss and his Work* (London: Dobson).

Crawford, D. W. (1974), *Kant's Aesthetic Theory* (Wisconsin: University Press).

Curl, G. F. (1973), 'Aesthetic judgments in dance', *Collected Papers in Dance*, Vol. 1. (Dance Section, Association of Teachers in Colleges and Departments of Education), 20–31.

Danto, A. (1964), 'The artworld', reprinted in (ed.) J. Margolis, *Philosophy Looks at the Arts* (2nd ed.).

Danto, A. (1973), 'Artworks and real things', *Theoria*, XXXIX, 1–17.

De Quincey, T., 'On murder considered as one of the fine arts', reprinted in (ed.) W. Peacock, *Selected English Essays* (London: University Press, 1903).

Dickie, G. (1964), 'The myth of the aesthetic attitude', reprinted in (ed.) J. Hospers, *Introductory Readings in Aesthetics* (New York: Macmillan, 1969).

Dickie, G. (1969), 'Defining art', reprinted in (ed.) M. Lipman, *Contemporary Aesthetics* (Boston: Houghton Mifflin).

Dickie, G. (1971), *Aesthetics: An Introduction* (New York: Pegasus Press).

Dickie, G. (1974), *Art and the Aesthetic: An Institutional Analysis* (New York: Cornell University Press).

Dickie, G. (1976), 'What is art?', in (ed.) L. Aagaard-Mogensen, *Culture and Art*.

Diffey, T. J. (1967), 'Evaluation and aesthetic appraisals', *BJA*, 7, 358–373.

Diffey, T. J. (1969), 'The republic of art', *BJA*, 9, 145–156.

Diffey, T. J. (1973), 'Essentialism and the definition of "art" ', *BJA*, 13, 103–120.

Diffey, T. J. (1975), 'Morality and literary criticism', *JAAC*, XXXIII, 443–454.

Diffey, T. J. (1977), 'The idea of art', *BJA*, 17, 122–128.

Diffey, T. J. (1977), 'A place for works of art', *Ratio*, XIX, 13–23.

Diffey, T. J. (1979), 'On defining art', *BJA*, 19, 16–23.

Ducasse, C. J. (1929), *The Philosophy of Art* (reprinted, New York: Dover Publications, 1966).

Dufrenne, M. (1972), Commentary on R. K. Elliott's 'The critic and the lover of art', in (ed.) W. Mays & S. C. Brown, *Linguistic Analysis and Phenomenology* (London: Macmillan).

Eliot, T. S. (1962), 'Literature and society', in *The Common Pursuit* (Penguin Books).

Elliott, R. K. (1972), 'The critic and the lover of art', in (ed.) W. Mays & S. C. Brown, *Linguistic Analysis and Phenomenology*.

Elliott, R. K. (1967), 'Aesthetic theory and the experience of art', reprinted in (ed.) H. Osborne, *Aesthetics* (London: OUP, 1972).

Elliott, R. K. (1973), 'Imagination in the experience of art', in *Philosophy and the Arts: Royal Institute of Philosophy Lectures*.

Elliott, R. K. (1974), 'Education, love of one's subject and the love of truth', *Philosophy of Education Society Proceedings*, VIII, 135–153.

Else, G. F. (1967), *Aristotle's Poetics* (Cambridge, Mass.: Harvard University Press).

Furlong, E. J. (1961), *Imagination* (London: Allen & Unwin).

Gallie, W. B. (1948), 'The function of philosophical aesthetics', reprinted in (ed.) W. Elton, *Aesthetics and Language* (Oxford, Blackwell, 1954).

Gallie, W. B. (1956), 'Essentially contested concepts', *PAS*, LVI, 167–198.

Gallie, W. B. (1956), 'Art as an essentially contested concept', *Philosophical Quarterly*, 6, 97–114.

Goodman, N. (1968), *Languages of Art* (London: OUP).

Griffiths, A. P. (1965), 'A deduction of universities', in (ed.) R. Archambault, *Philosophical Analysis and Education* (London: Routledge & Kegan Paul).

Hampshire, S. (1952), 'Logic and appreciation', reprinted in (ed.) W. Elton, *Aesthetics and Language*.

Hawkins, E. (1966), 'Pure poetry', in (ed.) S. J. Cohen, *The Modern Dance: Seven Statements of Belief*.

Hepburn, R. W. (1966), 'Contemporary aesthetics and the neglect of natural beauty', in (eds.) B. Williams & A. Montefiore, *British Analytic Philosophy* (London: Routledge & Kegan Paul).

Hirst, P. H. (1965), 'Liberal education and the nature of knowledge', in (ed.) R. Archambault, *Philosophical Analysis and Education*.

Hospers, J. (1956), *An Introduction to Philosophical Analysis* (London: Routledge & Kegan Paul).

Huizinga, J. (1944), *Homo Ludens: A Study of the Play Element in Culture* (English trans., Boston: Beacon Press, 1955).

Humble, P. N. (1982), 'Duchamp's Readymades: art and anti-art', *BJA*, 22, 52–64.

Hungerland, I. C. (1968), 'Once again, aesthetic and non-aesthetic', reprinted in (ed.) H. Osborne, *Aesthetics*.

Hunter, J. F. M. (1968), ' "Forms of life" in Wittgenstein's *Philosophical Investigations*', *APQ*, 5, 233–243.

Dance, art and aesthetics

Isenberg, A. (1949), 'Critical communication', reprinted in (ed.) W. Elton, *Aesthetics and Language*.
Iwanska, A. (1971), 'Without art', *BJA*, 11, 402–411.
Johnson, R. V. (1969), *Aestheticism* (London: Methuen).
Jones, P. (1969), 'Understanding a work of art', *BJA*, 9, 128–144.
Jones, P. (1975), *Philosophy and the Novel* (Oxford: Clarendon Press).
Jowitt, D. (1977), *Dance Beat: Selected Views and Reviews, 1967–1976* (New York and Basel: Marcel Dekker, Inc.).
Kant, I. (1790), *Critique of Judgment* (translated J. H. Bernard, New York: Hafner, 1972).
Kennick, W. (1958), 'Does traditional aesthetics rest on a mistake?', reprinted in (ed.) C. Barrett, *Collected Papers on Aesthetics* (Oxford: Blackwell, 1965).
Kosuth, J. (1969), 'Art after philosophy', *Studio International*, Oct., 134–137.
Kristeller, P. O. (1951), 'The modern system of the arts, Pt. 1', *Journal of the History of Ideas*, XII, 496–527.
Kristeller, P. O. (1952), 'The modern system of the arts, Pt. 2', *Journal of the History of Ideas*, XIII, 17–46.
Laban, R. (1960), *Mastery of Movement* (ed. L. Ullmann, London: Macdonald & Evans).
Langer, S. K. (1953), *Feeling and Form* (London: Routledge & Kegan Paul).
Langer, S. K. (1957), *Problems of Art* (London: Routledge & Kegan Paul).
Locke, J. (1690), *An Essay Concerning Human Understanding* (ed. J. W. Yolton, London: Dent, 1961).
Lyas, C. (1972), 'Aesthetic and personal qualities', *PAS*, LXXIII, 171–193.
Lyas, C. (1973), 'Personal qualities and the intentional fallacy', in *Philosophy and the Arts: Royal Institute of Philosophy Lectures*.
Lyas, C. (1976), 'Danto and Dickie on art', in (ed.) L. Aagaard-Mogensen, *Culture and Art*.
Lyas, C. (1981), Review of *Contemporary Aesthetics in Scandinavia*, *BJA*, 21, 268–271.
Macdonald, M. (1949), 'Some distinctive features of arguments used in criticism of the arts', reprinted in (ed.) W. Elton, *Aesthetics and Language*.
Macdonald, M. (1955), Review of *Feeling and Form*, *Mind*, LXIV, 549–553.
Mandelbaum, M. (1965), 'Family relationships and generalisations concerning the arts', *APQ*, 2, 219–228.
Margolis, J. (1976), 'Robust relativism', reprinted in (ed.) J. Margolis, *Philosophy Looks at the Arts* (2nd edn.).
Martin, J. (1933), *The Modern Dance* (reprinted, New York: Dance Horizons, 1965).
Martin, J. (1965), *Introduction to the Dance* (New York: Dance Horizons).
McFee, G. (1978), *Much of Jackson Pollock is Vivid Wallpaper: an essay in the epistemology of aesthetic judgements* (Washington: University Press of America).
McGregor, R. (1977), 'Dickie's institutionalised aesthetic', *BJA*, 17, 3–13.
Meager, R. (1958), 'The uniqueness of a work of art', reprinted in (ed.) C. Barrett, *Collected Papers on Aesthetics*.
Meager, R. (1970), 'Aesthetic concepts', *BJA*, 10, 303–322.
Meager, R. (1974), 'Art and beauty', *BJA*, 14, 99–105.
Moore, G. E. (1903), *Principia Ethica* (London: CUP).
Murdoch, I. (1970), *The Sovereignty of Good* (London: Routledge & Kegan Paul).
Oakeshott, M. (1962), 'The voice of poetry in the conversation of mankind', in his *Rationalism in Politics and Other Essays* (London: Methuen).
O'Connor, D. J. (1957), *An Introduction to the Philosophy of Education* (London: Routledge & Kegan Paul).
Osborne, H. (1970), *The Art of Appreciation* (London: OUP).
Osborne, H. (1980), 'Aesthetic implications of conceptual art, happenings, etc.', *BJA*, 20, 6–22.
Pauly, H. (1967), 'Inside Kabuki: an experience in comparative aesthetics', *JAAC*, XXV, 293–305.
Peirce, C. S., *Collected Papers, 1931–1935* (ed.) C. Hartshorne and P. Weiss (Cambridge: Harvard University Press, 1939).
Plato, *The Apology*, translated W. H. D. Rouse, in (ed.) E. H. Warmington and P. G. Rouse, *Dialogues of Plato* (New York: Mentor Books, 1956).
Plato, *The Republic*, as above.
Pole, D. (1976), 'Art, imagination and Mr Scruton', *BJA*, 16, 195–209.
Redfern, H. B. (1973), *Concepts in Modern Educational Dance*, (reprinted, London: Dance Books, 1982).
Redfern, H. B. (1978), 'Aesthetic qualities in the dance and their significance in education',

unpublished Ph.D. thesis, University of Manchester.

Reid, L. A. (1961), *Ways of Knowledge and Experience* (London: Allen & Unwin).

Reid, L. A. (1969), *Meaning in the Arts* (London: Allen & Unwin).

Reid, L. A. (1970), 'Movement and meaning', *Laban Art of Movement Guild Magazine*, 45, 5–31.

Rhees, R. (1954), 'Can there be a private language?', reprinted in his *Discussions on Wittgenstein* (London: Routledge & Kegan Paul, 1970).

Robinson, R. (1954), *Definitions* (London: OUP).

Rogers, L. R. (1963), 'Sculptural thinking', reprinted in (ed.) H. Osborne, *Aesthetics and the Modern World* (London: Thames & Hudson, 1968).

Sachs, C. (1937), *World History of the Dance* (reprinted, New York: Norton, 1963).

Saw, R. (1970), *Aesthetics: An Introduction* (London: Macmillan).

Schaper, E. (1968), *Prelude to Aesthetics* (London: Allen & Unwin).

Schaper, E. (1979), *Studies in Kant's Aesthetics* (Edinburgh: University Press).

Schaper, E. (1983), 'The pleasures of taste', in (ed.) E. Schaper, *Pleasure, Preference and Value* (London: CUP).

Schaper, E. and Sibley, F. N. (1966), 'About taste', *BJA*, 6, 55–69.

Schiller, J. C. F. (1801), *On the Aesthetic Education of Man – in a Series of Letters* (translated and ed., E. M. Wilkinson and L. A. Willoughby, Oxford: Clarendon Press, 1967).

Sclafani, R. S. (1973), 'Artworks, art theory, and the artworld', *Theoria*, 39, 113–152.

Sclafani, R. S. (1975), 'The logical primitiveness of the concept of a work of art', *BJA*, 15, 14–28.

Scruton, R. (1973), 'Architectural aesthetics', *BJA*, 13, 327–345.

Scruton, R. (1974), *Art and Imagination* (London: Methuen).

Scruton, R. (1979). *The Aesthetics of Architecture* (London: Methuen).

Searle, J. R. (1969), *Speech Acts: An Essay in the Philosophy of Language* (London: CUP).

Sharpe, R. A. (1975), 'Hearing-as', *BJA*, 15, 217–225.

Sibley, F. N. (1959), 'Aesthetic concepts', reprinted in (ed.) J. Margolis, *Philosophy Looks at the Arts* (2nd ed.).

Sibley, F. N. (1959), 'Aesthetics and the looks of things', reprinted in (ed.) F. J. Coleman, *Contemporary Studies in Aesthetics* (New York: McGraw-Hill, 1968).

Sibley, F. N. (1963), 'Aesthetic concepts: a rejoinder', *Phil. Rev.*, LXXII, 79–83.

Sibley, F. N. (1965), 'Aesthetic and non-aesthetic', *Phil. Rev.*, LXXIV, 135–159.

Sibley, F. N. (1968), 'Objectivity and aesthetics', *ASSV*, XLII, 31–54.

Sibley, F. N. (1974), 'Particularity, art and evaluation', *ASSV*, XLVIII, 1–21.

Sircello, G. (1975), *A New Theory of Beauty* (Princeton: University Press).

Sparshott, F. E. (1963), *The Structure of Aesthetics* (London: Routledge & Kegan Paul).

Stevenson, C. L. (1938), 'Persuasive definitions', *Mind*, XLVII, 331–350.

Stolnitz, J. (1960), *Aesthetics and the Philosophy of Art Criticism* (Boston: Houghton Mifflin).

Stolnitz, J. (1961), 'On the origins of "aesthetic disinterestedness" ', *JAAC*, XX, 131–143.

Strawson, P. F. (1954), 'Wittgenstein's *Philosophical Investigations*', reprinted in (ed.) P. F. Strawson, *Freedom and Resentment* (London: Methuen, 1974).

Strawson, P. F. (1966), 'Aesthetic appraisal and works of art', reprinted in his *Freedom and Resentment*.

Tanner, M. (1968), 'Objectivity and aesthetics', *ASSV*, XLII, 55–72.

Tanner, M. (1977), 'Sentimentality', *PAS*, LXXVII, 127–147.

Tatarkiewicz, W. (1963), 'Classification of arts in antiquity', *Journal of the History of Ideas*, 24, 231–240.

Tatarkiewicz, W. (1971), 'What is art? The problem of definition today', *BJA*, 11, 134–153.

Urmson, J. O. (1957), 'What makes a situation aesthetic?' (reprinted in (ed.) J. Margolis, *Philosophy Looks at the Arts* (1st ed., New York: Scribners, 1962).

Walton, K. L. (1970), 'Categories of art', reprinted in (ed.) J. Margolis, *Philosophy Looks at the Arts* (2nd ed.).

Weitz, M. (1956), 'The role of theory in aesthetics', reprinted in (ed.) J. Margolis, *Philosophy Looks at the Arts* (2nd ed.).

Weston, M. (1975), 'How can we be moved by the fate of Anna Karenina?', *ASSV*, XLIX, 81–93.

Wigman, M. (1966), *The Language of Dance* (London: Macdonald & Evans).

Winch, P. (1958), *The Idea of a Social Science and its Relation to Philosophy* (London: Routledge & Kegan Paul).

Wittgenstein, L. (1921), *Tractatus Logico-Philosophicus*, translated D. F. Pears and B. F. McGuinness

(London: Routledge & Kegan Paul, 1961).

Wittgenstein, L. (1953), *Philosophical Investigations*, translated G. E. M. Anscombe (Oxford: Blackwell).

Wittgenstein, L. (1958), *The Blue and the Brown Books* (Oxford: Blackwell).

Wittgenstein, L. (1966), *Lectures and Conversations on Aesthetics, Psychology and Religious Belief* (ed.) C. Barrett (Oxford: Blackwell).

Wollheim, R. (1968), *Art and Its Objects* (2nd ed., with six supplementary essays, London: CUP, 1980).

Wollheim, R. (1973), *On Art and the Mind* (London: Allen Lane).

Wollheim, R. (1971), 'Philosophy and the arts', in (ed.) B. Magee, *Modern British Philosophy* (reprinted, Paladin Books, 1973).

Index

ritual -, 11, 21, 96; social aspects/ functions of -, 6, 15, 48; tap -, 21, 27, 114; understanding -, 16–20, 87 (see also Understanding artworks)

Dancer(s), 15, 16, 17, 41, 65–66, 67, 81, 86, 92, 97; male and female -, 115
Dancing, 16, 41, 46, 59, 66, 86
Danto, A., 31ff., 58, 59, 61, 62
Dark Elegies (Tudor), 98
De Quincey, T., 50
Death of art, 40, 42
Death and the Maiden Quarter (Schubert), 108
Deception, 92, 118; self-, 91, 118
Defining/definitions, 6, 10, 22ff., 33ff., 42, 59, 77; persuasive -, 24
Degree courses in dance, ch. 1 *passim*
Delusion, 91, 92
Descartes, R., 68fn.
Description(s) 70, 71, 73
Desire(s), 49, 52, 88 (see also Sensations)
Developing aesthetic awareness, 79, 101, 107; -a concept of art, 41
Dickie, G., 33ff., 52
Diffey, T. J., 5, 10, 24–25, 26, 28, 34, 35, 42, 45, 61
Disagreement(s), 111ff.
Disinterested contemplation, 13, 51, 52, 53, 62, 85ff.
Drama, 53, 65, 110
Ducasse, C. J., 92
Duchamp, M., 60–61
Duck-rabbit figure, 106, 107
Dufrenne, M., 39fn., 57

Education, ch. 1 *passim*; -and aesthetic interest/the arts, 20, 79, 101, 107 (see also Learning)
Eight Jelly Rolls (Tharp), 49
Eliot, T. S., 38
Elitism in art, 34
Elliott, R. K., 57, 74fn., 104, 110
Embrace Tiger and Return to Mountain (Tetley), 108
Emotion(s), 12, 15, 31, 49, 66, ch. 7 *passim*, 119 (see also Feeling(s))
Ends and means, 51, 88
Enjoyments, participant and spectator -, 87 (see also Pleasure)
Epistemology, 8, 9, 51
Essentialism (in art), 6, 22–26

Ethics, 8, 9 (see also Moral)
Evaluation, 53, ch. 7 *passim*, ch. 8 *passim*
Evaluative use of words, 28, 70ff.
Everyday language/speech, 26–28 (see also Ordinary language)
Evidence, 9, 68 (see also Reasons)
Excellence in art, 22, 24, 48, 89–90
Expectations (and art), 39, 56, 61, 77, 78, 86–87, 100
Experience(s), 54, 65, 80, 113; aesthetic -, ch. 5 *passim*, 66, 82, ch. 7, ch. 8 *passim*; firsthand -, 51, 73, 90; sensuous -, 65–66
Expression of emotion, 15, 31 (see also Feeling(s))
Expressive qualities, 65–67, 69

Family resemblance(s), 26, 39–31
Feeling(s), 12, 15, 25, 27, 54fn., 62, 69, 74, ch. 7 *passim*, 114, 115, 118–119
Fine art(s), 6, 11, 12, 47, 48, 56, 58, 114
Firsthand experience, 51, 73, 90
First-order features/qualities, 68, 69, 78, 104, 106, 107
Folk dance, 11, 21, 65, 114
'For itself'/'for its (their) own sake', 46, 48, 51, 53, 85, 91ff., 99
'Form', 23, 52, 93
Form(s), 5, 31, 51, 53, 85, 93ff.; 'estimate of -', 85; 'significant -', 23, 24, 29
'Form(s) of life', 32, 99
Formal features/qualities, 15, 24, 53, 65, 93
Fountain (Duchamp), 61
Four Minutes 33 seconds (Cage), 61
Freedom, -in aesthetic experience/art, 33, 92, 98, 102, 111
Fry, R., 24
Furlong, E. J., 92

Galileo, G., 68fn.
Gallie, W. B., 25, 26, 30, 43
Generalise/generalising, 23, 37fn., 42
German artists, 16
Gestalt qualities, 68, 69
Goodman, N., 19
Graham, M., 34, 59, 108
Grading, 45

Hamlet (Shakespeare), 17
Hampshire, S., 100–101
'Happenings', 22, 56